He's a man of the streets and his experiences there have provided him with the basis for most of his humor—scathing, biting, but always honest.

Richard Pryor—a true original, in every sense of the word.

RICHARD PRYOR
THE MAN BEHIND THE LAUGHTER

BY JOSEPH NAZEL

HOLLOWAY HOUSE PUBLISHING COMPANY
LOS ANGELES, CALIFORNIA

PUBLISHED BY
Holloway House Publishing Company
8060 Melrose Avenue
Los Angeles, California 90046
International Standard Book Number 0-87067-013-1
Printed in the United States of America

For my family

RICHARD PRYOR
THE MAN BEHIND THE LAUGHTER

Though you may see me holler,
And you may see me cry—
I'll be dogged, sweet baby,
If you gonna see me die.
                    —Langston Hughes

1

A light layer of smog blanketed the laid-back Southern California community of Northridge. The pale gray and stale blue sky was being laced heavily with burnt orange, growing purple in the gathering dark of early evening.

It was Monday, June 9, 1980, and for those who were keeping count, it was also the 219th day of captivity for 50 Americans in revolution-torn Iran.

Street traffic through the community had eased somewhat as the street lights winked on to signal the approach of darkness. Behind the ornate iron gates and high walls, Northridge residents, secure from outside dangers, settled down to what they were sure would be another uneventful Monday night.

A lone figure dashed from a low-slung mansion which

lay on the tree dotted land like a slumbering giant. Arms flailing at his sides, the figure wobbled toward the iron gates separating the mansion from the outside world. In a moment the frantic figure had pushed the gate open and was running, arms dangling like soggy noodles, head back, glazed eyes focused on the gathering dark, seeing *pain*.

The lone figure trotted east on tree-shrouded Parthenia Avenue, his feet chewing up the ground in tiny frantic bits, word-fragments burbling from his sagging mouth, along with cries of sheer agony.

A curious neighbor brushed aside his curtains, watched the lone black man rushing down Parthenia and put in a call to the police.

Delirious with pain the man turned south onto Hayvenhurst Avenue drawing curious stares from passersby momentarily caught off guard by the odd sight.

Immediately a woman stepped forward and recognized that the man was in pain. His brown shirt was in melted tatters as if it had been both burned and ripped. The dark flesh of his chest and arms were charred raw. She tried to help.

Drivers slowed and paced the running figure, leaning from their vehicles to plead with the injured man to stop so that they might help.

"I can't stop! I can't stop!" the frightened black man managed between shrieks of pain, "I'll die if I stop!"

"Did someone call an ambulance?" one of the concerned passersby pressed, trying to keep up with the running figure.

"Who is he?"

"What happened?"

Questions were fired in rapid volleys which went unanswered as the curious, the questioning, and the con-

12

cerned gravitated to the strange "piper" who led them along with is cries of agony.

"I can't stop! I'll die if I stop!"

They could not help but share his pain, his agony. They rushed along with him, beside him, around him, grimacing against ugly wounds that marred his brown skin.

"Please stop!" a woman called to him.

The man raced on, oblivious to all but the pain that gripped him, digging its sharp nails into his tender nerves deep enough to agonize without killing.

Richard Zielinski, Los Angeles police officer, and his partner were on routine patrol when they saw the "pathetic piper" leading his charges along Hayvenhurst Avenue. They swung their patrol car into the front of the parade.

The man suddenly stopped his forward progress. His legs working like sluggish pistons, he ran in place, faster now as the pain made its presence felt.

Officer Zielinski pushed his way from the squad car and rushed up to assist the injured man. The officer recognized the man's injuries as serious burns.

"He just exploded in flames," explained an aged black woman who rushed up to the officers out of breath.

"Auntie help me!" the black man screamed out and took off, jogging, babbling, shrieking.

Officer Zielinski told his partner to radio their location to the ambulance drivers then jogged after the pain-crazed man, trying unsuccessfully to coax him into stopping.

"I can't stop!" the injured man screamed. "I'll die if I stop!"

The officer wanted to help, knew that he would have

to help, but did not want to further injure the badly burned man. He continued to jog along, talking, encouraging the frenzied man until he caught sight of the Fire Department's rescue ambulance.

The uniformed men from the Fire Department's rescue team went into action realizing that the burned man needed immediate attention. As delicately as they could they constrained the injured man.

"C'mon, give me a second chance!" the black man screamed, trying to fight off his helpers. "I know I did wrong but I've got some good in me."

"Who is he talking to?" some asked.

"What wrong has he done?" other passersby joined in, craning their necks so that they might better see the action taking place on once-serene Chase Street.

"We're trying to help you, man," one of the men from the Fire Department team insisted as he struggled with the wild-eyed black man. "C'mon man, let us help you."

The black man looked to the woman he had called "Auntie" for help. She looked on with pained eyes and begged him to cooperate with the uniformed men.

"He's in shock," one of the team members said. "Be careful."

The uniformed men moved quickly, methodically, finally getting the better of the injured man and strapping him to a stretcher.

"C'mon, give me a second chance," the injured man screamed out as the ambulance lurched away from the curb and down Chase Street.

By 8:30 p.m., Richard Franklin Lennox Thomas Pryor, a funny man from Peoria, Illinois, who had a pronounced fondness for "snorting cocaine," was near death in the burn ward of Sherman Oaks Hospital with

14

burns over 50 of his body. He wasn't expected to live.

Like vultures some kept up a "death watch," sorting through Pryor's history for tasty bits and pieces from the corpses of things past in order to fashion a full-blown feast for those who grow fat on the carrion of "gossip."

The faithful, those who cared, kept a vigil for Pryor, "putting in emergency calls to God" in his behalf, secretly going through their personal recollections for reasons to justify God's involvement in the "cause to save Richard Pryor."

"What good had Richard Pryor ever done for anyone?"

"Wasn't he just another rich dope-fiend?"

"Wasn't he just another loud nigger who was overwhelmed by his own success?"

"Why would God, or anyone else for that matter, want to intervene in Pryor's behalf?"

Each Pryor loyalist found his or her own answers to the questions that plagued them all. And as they traced their way through the dusty halls of memory, they each found more and more reason why the 39-year-old comedian shoudl be given another chance to finish the work he had taken on.

Pryor's story, like all our stories, while impacted by seemingly larger, more sensational historic events, was still a very integral part of that larger body of history and it is this impact that gives worth and meaning to life, to an individual's passage through life.

A man's history is a compilation of facts. If a man is to be judged, it must be done with a clear and accurate appraisal of history.

Once upon a time the pig drank wine
And the monkey got hung from the
streetcar line on . . .

2

Chapter 2: Jump Street!

"If you're born black, you come from Jump Street. I wonder if the doctors don't mess with you when you're born. And diseases!—especially if you're poor in this country. You live around rats and roaches and you survive those bites and don't get rabies when everybody in the world gets rabies, and you don't get brain damage from eating the lead paint. You come up and go to school and in spite of them trying not to teach you anything and destroy your character, you hold on to it and try to have your principles about you, and you learn all their stuff and hold yours and you're a proud black person walking the street. It's amazing! It knocks me out! It makes me cry."

Jump Street for Richard Franklin Lennox Thomas Pryor was North Washington Street in Peoria, Illinois, on December 1, 1940. Peoria was a town of 105,000 souls, the population swollen over the years by a rag-tag group of escapees from the deep South.

Seeking freedom from the racist practices in the South, the hopeful refugees looked northward and rushed the Mason-Dixon Line, pushing past the great Cotton Curtain which they were sure was the only thing separating them from a more human and prosperous reality. They got tricked.

Some found North Washington Street in Peoria. For others there was Lenox Avenue which knifes through New York City's Harlem. There was Filmore Street in San Francisco. Central Avenue in Los Angeles. Main and Division Streets in Biloxi, Mississippi. Howard Street. 116th Street. Beale Street.

The streets were the same, charged by the same energies, choked by the same miseries. But that was the beauty of the experience—sometimes. It created the Blues.

The street transcended reality and became a symbol for the vibrant culture that sprang from the masses of blacks who huddled on the banks of the rutted arteries.

Paule Marshall introduces the symbol in her work, *Brown Girl, Brownstones*: "Fulton Street . . . was clamorous voices, hooted laughter and curses ripping the night's warm cloak; a welter of dark faces and gold etched teeth; children crying high among the fire escapes of the tenements; the unrelenting wail of a blues spilling from a bar; a man and a woman in a hallway bedroom; a drunken woman pitching along the street; the sustained shriek of a police siren and its red light stabbing nervously at faces and window. Fulton Street on Saturday night was all beauty and desperation and sadness."

The street did not respect class or education. It was

fashioned as a place to tuck black folks away and out of sight. Whites did not differentiate between black folks. They, like their streets and neighborhoods, were all the same.

"Respectable tenants," writes Ann Petry in her 1940s novel, *The Street*, "in these houses where colored people were allowed to live included anyone who could pay the rent, so some of them would be drunk and loud-mouthed and quarrelsome given to fits of depression when they would curse and cry violently, given to fits of equally violent elation. And . . . because the walls would be flimsy, why, the people, the bad people, the children, the dogs, and the god awful smells would all be wrapped up together in one big package."

Street people who made their way in the streets, were not the same as those who lived on the street, their thoughts on that day when they would escape the street, escape the *niggerness* associated with the street, the blues, crime, drugs.

The lives of all who lived in, or on, the ghetto streets throughout America were all "wrapped up together in one big package." Their common fate was due to a similarity in condition. It was a forced similarity, visited on the "packaged" people by outsiders.

In the streets a black man learns what it is to be a man, a black man, not born nigger, or to be nigger. Nigger is a learned-in absurdity. Nigger is carefully and brutally orchestrated into the language, into tradition, into law and into reality by white folks using exclusion, poverty, undereducation, and even murder to insure that the process takes place or takes its toll. It is in the streets beyond his own street that he really feels his *niggerness* most of all, if he has not found some identity he can hold onto in his own streets.

21

Black militant H. Rap Brown, who managed to shake macho Americans with his call for black people to arm and protect themselves said, "The street is where young bloods get their education. I learned how to talk in the street, not from reading about Dick and Jane going to the zoo and all that simple shit. The teacher would test our vocabulary each week but we knew the vocabulary we needed. They'd give us arithmetic to exercise our minds. Hell, we exercised our minds by playing the Dozens."

Life in the streets was based on a different set of rules, different goals. "It was hard," Pryor said of his early years in the streets. "They (parents) did the best they could. They taught me stuff that the average person doesn't get to learn, like real morals and honesty and dignity. You have to have that if you're going to live in the streets. Your word is all you have."

What kind of morality can be found in the streets? Is it simply a reversal of definitions? Bad is now good, as African writer Dugmore Boetie sees the ghetto, "the skeleton with the permanent grin? A live carcass bloated with grief and happiness. Where decency was found in filth and beauty hidden behind ugliness. Where vice was virtue and virtue a vice. A Black heaven glowing with sparks of hell."

Pryor says of Peoria, "some of the neighborhoods, they called them 'bring your hat' neighborhoods 'cause they bring your hat to you. You go down there with your hat on and then later they hand it to you with your head in it . . . It's on the weekends a lot of that shit happens. People get drunk and it's like a pressure cooker, and then there are the fights."

Still, Pryor could tell an interviewer, "I see God in the streets. He's in me and around me."

Where is the morality?

"I used to be the neighborhood baby," Pryor explained to an interviewer for *Ebony* Magazine. "This one would take care of me while that one was out of town and like that. Then my grandmother started taking care of me. I always felt," he goes on, "I was the child protege of the neighborhood because they wouldn't let me get into stuff. No dope! I first smoked a reefer when I was twenty-years-old. I was that kind of child. They just seemed to help me all the time."

Is it possible that Pryor is leg-pulling when he boasts about his family, "We were *affluent*—had the largest whorehouse in the neighborhood."

And certainly Pryor is stretching the truth when he brags, "My grandmother. She was the madam. We had three on one block—313, 317 and 324 North Washington. My grandmother was the rule, the power base, a very strong woman."

If true, that would account for some of the characters and experiences that have entertained and shocked Pryor audiences. If not true it wouldn't discount the authenticity of Pryor's material because it is known that his grandmother owned and operated a pool hall in Peoria, up until her death, a recreation room for pimps and hustlers.

But Pryor insists that the whorehouse was a very real part of his life, along with other hardships. "I just saw some hard things in my life that I hope my kids don't have to see; my father fighting my mother, my being in the whorehouse . . . " But Pryor feels no shame. "On the other hand, I wouldn't change it. I think you live your life and there's something very, very special about it."

Pryor saw beauty in a wino trying to straighten out a

23

young junkie: "Boy, you know what your problem is? You don't know how to deal with the white man. I do, that's why I'm in the position I am in today." Maybe the irony is not intentional on the part of the wino who Pryor has allowed to show impotence in his failure to control the traffic on his *own* street, in his own neighborhood. Does it matter? Does it soften the sting of the tragic underlying truth?

"I always have a tendency," says Pryor, "to lean into the underlayers and tones of what people really are feeling."

Does Mudbone, the wino, feel his impotence? Has he recognized that he is considered a failure? Does he agree? And if he does see himself as a failure wouldn't that nullify anything he might say as being simply ramblings?

Not for Pryor. "Everybody got some good shit in 'em, you know, we *do*. I believe people good."

Is Pryor searching for an out? Is he trying to justify some of his eccentricities by weighing them against a good that is in all mankind?

"I mess up a great deal in my life," Pryor says. "But I do an enormous amount of good work that supercedes all the bullshit I go through."

More probably Pryor's perception was determined by the lessons he learned under his grandmother's care and in the streets themselves.

"My grandmother," said Pryor, "always told me, 'Son, one thing a white man can't take from you is the knowledge.' You take some sixty-three-year-old cat on the street, ugly, spit coming out his mouth, he's still got something you can't have. You can't say he didn't see that gutter or he didn't drink this wine. That is the knowledge."

The "knowledge" taken one step further, organized by a creative hand, becomes the art, the culture, the history and hopes of a people. It is what makes life "something very, very special."

The knowledge is translated into the language of the people and is thereby preserved and communicated in a more beautiful form by the artists.

"The language of the Negro," according to writer Sarah Webster Fabio, "is classical in the sense that it never gets too far from concrete realities, from the "thingy" quality of objects, persons, places, matter perceived."

Fabio explains further that "Negro . . . is a language—largely unassimilated and unlettered—which cuts through, penetrates things as they are reflected in spirituals, blues or jazz lyrics to a core of meaning eliciting a soulful response, to a moment of realization of what it means to be a human being in a world with a stranglehold on this awareness."

It was in the streets that Pryor learned to speak. He seldom reads but has noted that he remembers everything, including the mental and physical nuances of what is said to him. It explains his ability to capture, so quickly and easily, those living persons who give body to his humor, his art.

Lawrence Levine observed, "Black humor . . . presupposed a common experience between the joke-teller and the audience. Black humor, too, transformed personal expression into collective expression. Black humor, too, functioned to foster a sense of particularity and group identification by widening the gap between those within and those outside of the circle of laughter."

While Pryor's humor, black in content and context,

does not appeal readily to white sensibilities, the art of it transcends the uneasy feelings and reaches that level of universality when all parties are unmasked for what they are.

Pryor has become a universal artist, though many would deny that anything black could ever have a universal impact.

Pryor's art, like black music, can easily reach out to others because of its very visual quality which combines with vocals which are qualified by tones, sounds that communicate without use of the spoken word.

It is truly the language which has come from the streets. And that language is spoken and acted out with a series of nods, movements of the face, eyes and hands, vocal inflections which take away all doubt as to what is meant. The language, like Pryor's comedy, must be seen and heard at the same time in order to be fully understood. A movement of the eyes can change the entire meaning of a word or phrase. A change in pitch can be a warning, even in the most innocent of conversations.

Part of Pryor's act is a routine where he says, "I feel," without much feeling inititially. But in a matter of moments, using the same "I feel," his change in inflection and facial and body movements transform the word into a living piece of art that expresses pain, pleasure, agony, a series of emotions carefully orchestrated by Richard Pryor.

It is universal because it is universally understood. It is universal not because it looks exactly like art forms or statements from other cultures but because it serves the same *function*. A foot does the same job no matter the color.

"Niggers just have a way of telling you stuff," said Pryor, "and not telling you stuff. Martians would have a difficult time with niggers. They be translating words, saying a whole lot of things underneath you, all around you. That's our comedy." More to the point it is reflective of all arts which came out of the black experience—blues, jazz, even the literature, though Amiri Baraka (Leroi Jones) would disagree, at least where literature is concerned.

" . . . the absence of achievement," writes Baraka, who was a thorn in the side of both the black middle class and the white establishment, "among serious Negro artists, except in Negro music, is that in most cases the Negroes who found themselves in a position to pursue some art, especially the art of literature, have been members of the Negro middle class, a group that has always gone out of its way to cultivate *any* mediocrity, as long as that mediocrity was guaranteed to prove to America, and recently to the world at large, that they were not really who they were, i.e., Negroes."

Poet Langston Hughes echoed Jones, writing that "this is the mountain standing in the way of any true Negro art in America—this urge within the race toward whiteness, the desire to pour racial individuality into the mold of American standardization, and to be as little Negro and as much American as possible."

The underlying assumption is that in order to be "American" blacks must mimick whites in thought, word and deed. This was something that street people objected to, rebelled against. It was this kind of rebelliousness that was *learned* into Pryor through his association with those blacks who made up that body.

Pryor is reluctant to give too many details about his early life, in the streets, in the whorehouse. It is what he calls his "real stuff" which he protects with the passion and concern with which one would watch over the family jewels.

But there is no doubt that Pryor, like most black young men facing puberty in the late forties and early fifties, knew what it was to hang on the corner.

Corner boys knew where the action was. At least they watched, listened, muscle-flexing as they "began to smell themselves good," as the old folks say.

On the corner young blacks got the message of who they were, who they might have been and might be. It was on the corner that they heard the blues "talkin' shit" and "teachin' " from the dark, smokey innards of bars. On the corner they saw the world, as they knew it, and all its nuances. It was a living encyclopedia that kept an account of history through song and a rich folk poetry, toasts, which comprised the oral tradition that kept things *alive*.

The oral tradition is a very personalized way of communicating thoughts and ideas.

The Dozens, toasts, jokes were all part of the oral tradition and were games street corner boys got into to pass time. "It's like niggers train in a different way," said Pryor. "Like, they don't have no theater groups, but niggers train on the corner, you know what I mean? Like when you hang out bullshittin', and singin' and shit. I mean, them cats trainin' for when they get their groups together."

Pryor would have been exposed to the stories told by pimps, hustlers and gamblers. He would have been exposed to the toasts which bragged of black victories over whites, passed on information or simply entertained.

The signifying monkey toast is one of the better known, revolving around the antics of a fast talking monkey who cons a lion into fighting an elephant:

The Monkey told the Lion one bright summer
day,
"There's a bad motherfucker heading your way.
"He talked about you brother, put your sister in
the shelf,
"The way he talked about your mother I wouldn't
say to myself."
The lion is forced to defend himself and his against
the slurs of the "dozens" playing elephant without
challenging the signifying monkey's accusations. It ends
in disaster for the lion, who finally says "quits."
The "signifier" becomes the target of the angry Lion.
"Said, "Monkey, I'm not kickin' your ass for
lyin',
I'm kicking your hairy ass for signifyin'."
But the quick-thinking monkey is up for the
challenge, his mind working against the Lion's brawn,
first failing in a teary appeal to the Lion's sympathy,
then attacking the Lion's macho:
The Monkey said, "Let me get my teeth out of the
grit and my balls out of the sand,
and I'll fight your ass like a *real* he-man."
So the Lion stepped back to the end of the curve,
'cause that was the boldest challenge he'd ever
heard.
But faster than the hand or the human eye could
see.
.the Monkey was back in the coconut tree.
Bruce Jackson did a great deal of research into the
street toast and concluded in his book, *Get Your ass in
the Water and Swim Like Me*, the toast is a kind of
street theater, a theater involving only one performer at
a time. People who can say the lines but cannot act them

get little opportunity to perform, because they are boring."

Jackson adds further, "The streetcorner world includes those who make it with brawn and those who make it with brains, and a very few who make it with both."

Pryor found out early that he wasn't a street-fighter. "I would always get degraded in a fight. Yeah, I wanted to win them all, but the dude would make me back down and I would always feel like a coward. I'd go home and say, 'Nigger, if you are a coward then stay out of those situations and you won't have to worry about it.' Then I'd find a little something to make me feel cool."

Pryor admitted that he once "used to take a lot of drugs—to experiment, to find out who I was. Mostly I did it to accept the fact that I was no street-fighter."

In that respect the streets of Peoria's black community were much the same as the other streets in ghettos around the United States. They were angry places. Places where a man, or a woman, could get killed, sometimes, over the slightest provocation. When you could not run—even "cool run," like Richard—you had to learn to survive, or be broken. Pryor learned that early. His characters reflect that realization. They know their limits. Many of them constantly, though slyly, challenge those limits at every opportunity.

It was through humor that blacks challenged those limits and taboos imposed on them. The humor was biting, showing a situation for being absurd, yet there was an undercurrent, the recognition that pushing the limits too far could lead to an ass whuppin', or worse.

Here we find the essence of Pryor's sharp humor. It cuts both ways, like a swinging pendulum, punishing

30

both, unmasking all the participants in the tragi-comedy. There is nothing more tragic or funny than Pryor's confrontation with the reality of the awesome power of the police in his role as Oilwell who asserts that he is "six-foot-five, four hundred and twenty pounds of *maaaaaaannn*!"

The assertion is always applauded by all within ear-shot. The act is a defiant one. A show of strength. But there are consequences which have to be faced. The act could be suicidal. Confrontations with police are often degrading.

"Boy, you hit me with that stick I'm gonna bite your dick! They'll be some bloodshed. I ain't bullshittin'."

Or Jesse who would fight the cops.

Cop: You kids stop having so much fun and go home.

Jesse: I ain't goin' no place.

Cop: We've got ways of making you move.

Jesse: Yeah, well they'd better be some good ones.

The defiance would lead to a battle with 30 cops who issue Jesse what is referred to in the streets sometimes as a very "righteous ass whuppin'."

It was a bitter victory for Jesse. And it is still a victory, even though he is viciously beaten. For Pryor's people the victory comes in Jesse's willingness to stand his ground no matter the consequences. He becomes the absurd heroic figure who is celebrated in his defeat. No one expected things to be otherwise, though in the back of their minds, way back so as not to be a pressure, they hoped that Jesse would win out, for them all.

Pryor is no Jesse or Oilwell. He gave up that hope when he claims to have been "unmasked" for the coward he supposedly was by a stern, "Nigger! Unball your fist!" Pryor backed down!

Oddly, though, he hasn't backed down from much

since. He found, like most other brothers who onced *do whopped* with the "corner brigade," that there were many more ways of getting over and surviving life in the streets. Being cool, quick-witted and using his keen perception to put things together, Pryor survived, as the Signifying Monkey did, with guile.

"We used to have good sessions sometimes," Pryor said of the verbal contests, "I remember once I came up with a beaut, man, I killed them one day. We was doin' it all day to each other, you know. Bang-bang—'Your shoes are run over so much, look like your *ankles* is broke,' and shit like that. I called the motherfucker 'The Rummage Sale Ranger,' you know what I mean? 'Cause that's where he got his clothes. That was a knockout, I saved that one for the last, that ended it."

Like the Dozens, the word games, the jibes and jokes, were not intended to draw blood. They were intended as insulation against the depression that came with the realization that the joke-teller was in the same boat as the butt of his joke.

"Under the mask of humor," says Gershon Legman, psychologist, "our society allows infinite aggressions, by everyone and against everyone."

It was the tool most often used by slaves who found some satisfaction in humor that sliced out at their oppressors without any fatal consequences. Still, there were fights.

Pryor became a master of the art, learning how to overcome the obstacles he faced, so that he wouldn't have to run. In the late forties and in the fifties, there really wasn't any place to run. His ancestors had already run from segragation in the South to meet a more subtle kind in Peoria.

But for all of Pryor's energy it is doubtful that this

talent would have developed beyond the level of the streets and small time bars if not for the encouragement of one Juliette Whittaker, supervisor of the Carver Community Center in Peoria.

The Carver Community Center, like most of its kind, were buffers provided by the white community. Part of their function was to limit gang fights, supposedly due only to idleness.

Richard Wright saw the sometimes folly in them and wrote, "They were paying me to distract . . . with ping-pong, checkers, swimming, marbles, and baseball in order that he might not roam the streets and harm the valuable white property which adjoined the black belt." But Wright did not damn the "clubs and ping-pong as such," pointing out that "these little stopgaps were utterly inadequate to fill up the centuries-long chasm of emptiness which American civilization had created . . . I felt that I was doing a kind of dressed-up police work, and I hated it."

Juliette Whittaker took her work seriously and helped Pryor direct his energy. At age twelve Pryor made his first appearance at Carver Community Center. He played the King in the Center's production of *Rumpelstiltskin*. The role became a trademark routine when Pryor took to the professional stage.

In 1977 Pryor returned to Peoria and in a show of everlasting gratitude presented Juliette Whittaker with the Emmy statuette he won for writing a Lily Tomlin special. Pryor hadn't forgotten those who helped him. It is a trait that shines through all the jive that often clouds the mystique of the man.

But the early years were not always street-corner fingerpoppin', Dozens games and basketball. There was school. And though school, before the May 17, 1954 legislation that was supposed to knock down *separate but equal* educational institutions, was quite different, the difference was hardly a positive one.

Pryor's inititial exposure to the school system was as a Catholic. "I went to Catholic school for about three weeks," Pryor told David Felton of *Rolling Stone*, "and then somebody said that my mother worked in a whorehouse, you know, so I got kicked out of school. It was a drag, 'cause that was the only school I was gettin' good grades in. They were very polite! It's not enough that he's a nigger, but you see . . .' "

Pryor's mother, Gertrude, was a Catholic and Pryor was born in a Catholic hospital, quipping, "I was born in St. Francis Hospital—I was meant to be a Catholic, you know. That was pretty hip to be born in a hospital in Peoria. Most cats was born at home, in the kitchen."

The remainder of his school career was spent in the public school system in Peoria. Probably a good thing for the Catholic Church. Pryor's sensitivity and intensity might well have led him into the priesthood. Given Pryor's attitudes and approaches to things, the Vatican would have had its hands full.

Allegedly Pryor was put into a class for the mentally retarded because of his hyperactivity. Absurd? Of course! But it was reflective of the times. Teachers were not expected to be sensitive to the children of the darker herd that crowded into the cities. And even those few who were sincerely concerned about educating their charges found it difficult, at times, to communicate because of the very real cultural gap that separates the black community from the white community.

Pryor would have a rougher time of it. He would have faced the school system that had not heard of the still un-inked *Brown vs Topeka, Kansas School Board*. All studies of the time were directed at finding out just why *they* supposedly could not compete with their white counterparts. Even some black escapees supported such "victim-directed" dissections that were designed to support the assumption that blacks were either inherently inferior to whites, or that they were inferior to whites because of the long years of slavery and poverty and racism that kept them separated from mainstream America. In any case, liberals and racists seemed to agree on one thing: black folks, at least most—Roy Wilkins was cool—were inferior *but it really wasn't their own fault*.

Pryor had established a "rep" as a prankster. It is no doubt that this show of embryonic genius was probably misread by those who still had not accepted blacks as possessing a distinctly black culture, even though they were interacting with the larger group.

Pryor was expelled at age fourteen for hitting a science teacher. Did the confrontation come out of a need for better communication? It's hard to tell. But it is certain that by then Pryor had begun to feel his *niggerness*, or at least the illfitting jacket of niggerness that was being forced on his still growing mind and body.

"When I was a little boy," said Pryor, "I was in love with this girl in my class, and I brought her a scratch board. You know, one of those gray cardboard things you draw on, and then you lift up the plastic and the picture's gone? The next day her daddy comes to school and says, 'Don't you dare give my little girl a present.' When I told my father he just shook his head. You see, nobody had told me about racism, but he knew!"

Pryor's father, Leroy, owned a construction company in Peoria. As a young adult Pryor is said to have driven a truck for his father. It would be difficult to guess at the elder Pryor's reasons for not telling his son about racism, though it is a subject which is more difficult to explain to a youngster than is the whole matter of creation and sex. There is a logic to sex, a simplicity that follows. Where is the logic in racism?

Maybe we can find the answer in Pryor's art. Or at least get an overview of the chaos, racism, that hit Pryor without warning, a jolt that all blacks have faced. Pryor would have had to find some way to deal with it humorously.

The wino who gets blamed for a break in the levee in Lawrence County provides a clue to how some parents, probably Pryor's, approached the whole subject of racism.

In defense of himself under the charge of allowing the levee to bust, the wino said, "Shit, can't a nigger in the world hold back no water when it want to go!" And explaining why he didn't run through the water to warn the people he says, "They was gonna find out about it soon enough.

All black children find out about racism "soon enough," which is often too soon. And many black parents, especially those who have escaped from the South where training is started much earlier, avoid the subject in hopes that they will never have to address themselves to the degarding aspects of their own participation in or lack of power over the madness.

"I was ready to cry as a kid," Pryor said, and explained that he, like all kids, saw things simply, without color. "I didn't think about color—just feelings. My heroes at the movies were the same as everyone else's. I wanted to be John Wayne too. I didn't know John Wayne hated my guts." Bubbles burst quickly. "That's

36

the way I see kids," said Pryor. "I just get fascinated talking to 'em, 'cause it'll be honestly sweet, and whatever they say is innocent. They deal with real shit."

Pryor survived it all; the whorehouse, the streets, the public school system. And a great deal of credit must be given to his grandmother Marie Carter Pryor Bryant who was the guiding force in Pryor's life, the "rule" which had to be obeyed.

Much of Pryor's defiance must have come from the independent Marie Bryant. If in fact she actually owned a chain of whorehouses, it would be proof that she lived in defiance of all the rules and regulations set to keep her in check. Still, all information seems to show that she refused to allow young Richard Pryor the same latitude, forcing him to conform to certain restrictions.

Pryor's mother died in 1969 but it was Pryor's grandmother who had taken over his upbringing long before. Pryor recalled his mother: "My mother went through a lot of hell behind me, because people would tell her, 'You don't take care of that boy.' She always wanted me to be somebody and she wasn't the strongest person in the world. But I give her a lot of credit. At least she didn't flush me down the toilet like some do."

While he was understanding of his mother's plight, he more than adored his strong-willed grandmother. In 1977 he bought her an expensive, ranch style home in Peoria. But she was only to enjoy the home for two years. Marie Bryant passed away in 1979 tearing some of the heart out of her adoring grandson.

Pryor was overwhelmed with grief at the passing of the one person who could still exercise some modicum of control over the "so-called" unpredictable Pryor. He had cancelled all of his concert dates when the seventy-nine-year-old, still-active businesswoman was felled by a stroke. He spent his time near her, and was with her when she died at 6:30 in the morning in Methodist Medical Center in Peoria.

Miss Mexcine Pryor, an aunt of the humorist's, was reported to have said of Pryor, "He just stood there shaking like a rag doll. He was just crying and talking, 'Mamma! Mamma! Mamma!' He had a grip on her hand and they couldn't pry him loose without a struggle. They couldn't get him out of that room and when they did, he broke and come right back in there.

"When they pulled him out of there and took him down to the lounge, that's when he really broke down. I tried to console him and he cried: 'Everything I've had and everything I've got is gone. My mamma's gone. I just loved her, I loved her, I loved her. Mamma, I did everything I could for you. Everything! I prayed, and I prayed. Mamma, I prayed so hard. I didn't even know I could pray.''

While alive Pryor's grandmother saw to it that he graduated from Central High School where it is said that he lettered as a cool running halfback, and as a center and forward in basketball.

There may still be some doubt as to the authenticity of reports by Pryor that he actually lived in a whorehouse. Pryor may well have concocted the story to further enhance the rebelliousness of his art as symbol. There is no doubt that Pryor loved and respected his grandmother, and, but for her, the Pryor story might well have taken a quite different course.

*Rabbit Philosophy: Don't trust a man,
he might have a dog in his pocket . . .*

Chapter 3: Street Nigger!

There is a difference in a Street Nigger and a Country Nigger who is just up from the South. It was especially so in the middle and late fifties and the early sixties. The cadences to which they danced were different under their umbrella of sameness.

Richard Pryor was a bona fide graduate of the streets—a Street Nigger. He learned how the white world saw him—or *did not* see him according to Ralph Ellison's Invisible Man—and he took more privileges, challenged more limits than his country counterpart.

People, black folks anyway, who were born and bred in the South under segregation, knew their limits, and knew what the consequences of trying to stretch those limits would be. They were still lynching black people in the South and getting away with it!

Rural blacks knew that to strike a white man would

be cause for death—immediate and unchallenged by law. The Street Nigger avoided confrontations with whites only when jobs were at stake. The jobless ones were not about to take any shit from the white man, with the possible exception of the local police.

When most Americans who are old enough take a nostalgic look back to the fifties and sixties, they somehow only see those supposedly "Happy Days" in a non-existent "Laverne and Shirley" world where crises that could not be handled by Ozzie and Harriet didn't exist. There was no Negro problem. How could there be? There were no Negroes! Well, maybe a *Kneegrow* or two, but no niggers!

Closer to the truth, a truth that America would probably rather forget, there were too many blacks, ah, Negroes—it was "before black was beautiful," according to Pryor. "You call somebody black in those days and the dude, he'd say, 'I don't play that! I ain't black, I'm a Negro.'"

It was that kind of world. Negroes were rising up and sitting down, without permission, in places where they did not have any business sitting down—according to the signs posted at any rate.

Things were happening. Blacks were developing a stiff left jab in the persons of aggressive young black people like Dr. Martin Luther King, Jr., who broke the back of the segregated Birmingham, Alabama, bus system; a then-young Andrew Young; and a young ex-criminal who had taken on a revolutionary brand of religion in coping with America, Malcolm X.

In 1958 Pryor volunteered for the draft and spent the next two years in the United States Army. Much of Pryor's army career was spent in Kaiserslautern, Germany.

Pryor told interviewer David Felton, "I gave some head for the first time in my life when I was in Germany. That was an experience. I'll never forget how it felt on my head, her pussy . . . her hairs and all . . . I knew I would be doing it again.'' According to Pryor, his newly acquired skills proved helpful in getting him gigs when he returned stateside. A stripper Pryor claims to have serviced saw to it that he worked steadily when he tried his hand at MCing in small clubs and bars.

Pryor had a couple of violent confrontations while in the army. Some critics like to point them out as examples of Pryor's volatile and unstable temper. Blacks who have spent any time in Uncle Sam's services might offer a great many tales of blacks having to get down and go to war with white folks who were trying to push that white supremacy game away from their own turf. Street niggers and Southern white supremacists are natural enemies!

Renee, Pryor's first child, was born in 1958. Three more would follow over the years.

Pryor survived his stint in the United States Army, finding time to appear in amateur variety shows during his hitch. Pryor was honorably discharged in 1960 and returned to the States and to Peoria where he was married.

America was in turmoil. The sixties opened with controversy which only compounded the ''Red threat'' paranoia that was keeping the manufacturers of personalized bomb shelters busy. The Negroes were on the move!

Southern blacks under new and aggressive leadership were confronting the Jim Crow system that had kept them in lock step for the duration of their stay in this country. It was not a back to Africa movement like that sponsored by Marcus Garvey in the early years of the Twentieth Century. No! The mood was a nonviolent one, at least on the part of the blacks who had taken to the streets to demand their rights under the United

States Constitution, bringing God in on their team, singing "We Shall Overcome" to the crack of billy clubs.

America's case of "Sputnikitis" did not foreshadow the steadily growing Civil Rights Movement. Television news found that it had better "action" simply by following the clashes of Negroes and police which were erupting throughout the South. At that time it was a predominantly Southern Movement. And though blacks in the North and West were aware of Dr. Martin Luther King, Jr. due to media exposure, their die was cast with the tried and true National Association for the Advancement of Colored People.

It was a time of discovery for the leaders of the Negro Movement. The great push spearheaded by King's newly founded Southern Christian Leadership Conference (SCLC) generated heated discussions on purpose and methodology. Negroes were probing those deeply seated differences in opinion that had never before had cause to pop to the surface.

It was a frightening time for those in the South. Travelling was like moving in occupied territory. The nation was constantly shocked by televised reports of violence being visited on their darker brethren but it all took place down South, a foreign country that had nothing to do with the white folks in the North. There were a few blacks who sat back on their *above-the-neckbone* haunches and "tish-tished" the antics of their country cousins who were actually setting the tone for what would happen to and for Negroes in America over the next two decades.

But it was essentially a Southern movement. It was the country black folk who had not managed to escape the strictures of the segregated South or pull themselves out of the muck of ignorance so that they might exercise their rights to vote. Northern blacks could vote, though too many of them didn't. It just wasn't their problem, although they sympathized, horrified by the violence, as were whites.

There was sympathy for the Southern movement but the Northern black had problems of his own. The long hot summers that ripped Detroit, Philly, Newark and Watts, were yet to happen. But the mood was still angry, smouldering. There were no jobs.

Pryor was a part of the street action. He was of the streets, by choice or by birth didn't matter. It was, in a sense, the only world Pryor knew. Pryor, like most street people, niggers as opposed to Negroes, was not nonviolent, and was not prepared to learn the art of nonviolence. This attitude—the inability or unwillingness to control responses to outward aggression, violent or otherwise—would follow Pryor the rest of his life, misread too often by critics who weren't able to face the truth—all heroes don't ride white horses!

Niggers were *talking shit* in the city streets trying to psyche themselves up for something. Many didn't know exactly what. It didn't matter. There were enough folks around who would give them something to believe in.

Negroes in the South were marching and praying and singing, confronting violence with brotherly love, a poor shield against a brick or bottle.

Young Negroes, the college brand, had risen up and started sitting down in places where Negroes had never been able to stand or walk before. And the Freedom Riders had gained national television exposure, further salting the American palate with fresh blood.

Pryor picked up the beat he danced to from the streets. It wasn't so much that he did not want the same things that his counterparts in the South wanted. He was not about to be nonviolent in order to show that he deserved them. And unlike the more "dichty" of the Negro race, Pryor was not about to clean himself up to the point where he was *acceptable*. It was part of a growing rebelliousness that did not impact Pryor alone. That same anger, spitefulness and hatred for whites was hardening the hearts of a great many young blacks who saw no future in playing up to white people.

Some folks were talking like there was going to be serious trouble in the streets of America if white people didn't get right and back off of black folks. One of those people talking was a young ex-con, Malcolm. It is rumored that Richard Pryor met Malcolm back in those early days when Malcolm was getting his own program together. If the rumor proves false it would not change the import of the suggestion of such a meeting. Pryor came out of the same environment. He would have met and rapped with a lot of Malcolms, black men who were raising questions and demanding change before the answers came.

"For a while I couldn't get a job nowhere except for about three clubs," said Pryor. "It was mostly pimps, whores, and junkies who liked me—the same people I was 'doing' onstage. They could relate."

Pryor recognized that the black middle-class, still grappling over whether they should adopt Negro or Afro-American as a racial identity to be slapped onto birth certificates and work applications, could never accept him. Not on his terms. Is it possible that a great deal of Pryor's refusal to "soften" or clean up his act was due to an early rejection by members of the so-called black middle class?

Pryor told David Felton, "A lot of niggers looked

down on us (because of his family's association with the whorehouse). But, also, when it came time for an election, all the political people would come to the whorehouse to try to win votes, to tell all the whores that there wouldn't be no busts and shit like that.''

It was the kind of time when a great many Negroes were looking for and manufacturing blacks, rather *Kneegrows* who would be a ''credit to the race'' before a court of white critics. Pryor was not a candidate. If anything Pryor was an example of what ''dichty'' folk would call ''one of *those* niggers!''

The cry was Freedom! but it meant integration, assimilation. At least so it seemed to angry young black folk who had found that they dug dancing to their own music. The rift was showing. The Negro Movement was splintering into many movements.

Poet Amiri Baraka—at that time known as Leroi Jones—caught the growing cadence of the time, writing:

> We want live words of the hip live flesh
> & coursing blood. Hearts Brains Souls
> splintering fire. We want poems like fists
> beating niggers out of jocks or dagger poems
> in the slimy bellies of the owner-jews—
> We want poems that kill.
> Assassin poems, poems that shoot guns.

Baraka was speaking for and to the people as poet. And if Malcolm X was prophet, leader, Pryor was social critic/entertainer—a one-man theater of the street.

It is doubtful that Pryor articulated his anger and rebelliousness in revolutionary terms. That is not the function of the rebel. He does not articulate, he responds to those energies which others will organize into formal thought.

Pryor could not have separated himself from the fury and chaos that surrounded his stage and private life. He couldn't separate the two lives. The pimps, whores, junkies, winos all related because Pryor had not only captured but become one with them—the Baad Niggers!

"Bad Niggers," wrote William H. Grier and Price M. Cobbs in *Black Rage,* "are feared as much by blacks as by whites . . . They are angry and hostile. They may seem at one moment meek and uncompromised and in the next a terrifying killer. Because of his experience in this country," Grier and Cobbs contend, "every black man harbors a potential bad nigger inside him. He must ignore this inner man. The bad niger is bad because he has been required to renounce his manhood to have his life (A theme that runs throughout Pryor's work).

"The bad nigger," they conclude, "is a defiant nigger, a reminder of what manhood could be."

But, as psychologist Joseph White points out, the bad nigger is only a "hero in the black community" while "white people continue to perceive this person as the villian."

It is little wonder that Pryor could only find employment as an MC in local dives. There was no market for his kind of niggerness either in the Negro world or the white.

"I don't want to be no Dick Gregory," Pryor said. "He's smarter than me. I don't like to read, for one thing, and I don't have the qualities to be an ambassador or nothing like that. My shit is more emotional, not intellectual like Dick Gregory."

What Pryor meant was that his shit is immediate, like all art that comes out of the oral tradition. It deals with now! It is upfront and live. And you, as participant or audience, don't have to bring anything to it, even imagination. That's provided through recognition, the ability of the audience to identify the characters being presented.

Ben Sidran remarked that "all oral communication is a *direct* reflection of the immediate environment and of the way in which members of the oral community relate that environment."

Pryor uses the language of the streets to reach the people of the streets. Though he claimed not to want to be an ambassador, read "credit to the race," which sets the so-called "heroic" figure up as an example of what the race can do if just given the opportunity. Pryor became just that. He was the "ambassador" for those people who "lived the backside of life and . . . saw things different."

One of Pryor's assets is the ablity to strike through to the core of things. It is simply that Pryor lerned early how to be deadly honest. "My father was devastatingly funny," Pryor told Maureen Orth of *Newsweek,* "and would tell the truth even if people didn't want to hear it." Pryor found that raw truth, if presented properly, could be funny and entertaining. It is the essence of his work.

Pryor is the mouth that roars, the Monkey that signifies, who speaks not for but through the very people who laugh. He strips away pretentions, as with the ineffective might of Oilwell, the worth of the liquor-soaked philosophy spluttered by Mudbone or of Macho Man's impotence. A sardonic irony.

"You have to know what the character went through . . . you have to have lived some life. You got to have paid some dues."

Pryor's dues paying started the day he first felt the lash of racism during his school days and picked up again in a Peoria dive called Harold's Club. It was Pryor's first professional gig. He played there until he stepped up to a $70-a-week gig.

The small time gigs and MCing jobs in small clubs continued and Richard Pryor slowly honed his act, paying dues, going hungry, maybe. He doesn't say much about those early years. One thing is certain, Pryor was never very far from the influence of the streets, something his critics feel is responsible for what they call his "emotional outbursts," "lack of discipline," and other so-called self-destructive tendencies which have caused him work, money, but certainly not exposure.

Pryor played the Faust Club in East St. Louis, the Shalimar in Buffalo, the Famous Door in Peoria, training in the minors.

While Pryor was playing "crazy," because he certainly had not paid enough dues to earn the title so early, Dick Gregory was doing a Mort Sahl on America, taking his work to the streets when he found that his stage routine wasn't enough to turn things around. Gregory took his work seriously, many think too seriously. Pryor was learning.

Another young comedian was on the set, working in the big time, a university graduate who would say, "I am interested in bettering the black man's image. I don't want to present him as a black man, but as a human being. . . . I want to do comedy. . . . I try to keep my humor away from the specific "black" and make it pertain to the general "human." Likewise, I want to make films and to play not a Negro, but human being." The young comedian who had captured America's heart and laugh track was Bill Cosby.

Pryor and Cosby were both about the same thing. Their methodology was different. Pryor was at war and painted his pictures with a warrior's brush, though applied with the style of an artist.

Cool Cos did much for the image of the black man on the screen. Unfortunately it changed little on the streets, just as blacks would realize twenty years later that the majority of Civil Rights legislation that had come down the river were just so many bits of yellowing parchment.

Pryor was quite different. Compared with Cool Cos and his characters, Fat Albert and Company, Pryor was a raging maniac, a fugitive from an insane asylum. Still, he had a certain something that lifted him from the honky tonks of Peoria to Greenwich Village in New York where he came to get over.

Paul Schrader, the director of "Blue Collar," said that Pryor "has a boyish quality that allows him to do or say almost anything and be forgiven. He can say things no other black man can get away with and a white audience will put up with it because his manner lessens the threat without diluting the message. Richard will be the biggest black star in history if he can keep the reins on himself or bite his tongue."

Schrader only echoed what many advisors laid on Pryor. But Pryor was not one who listened often, at least not to those who would have him be other than what he felt that he was.

Pryor could say what he wanted but he had better be very careful how he said it. Those were the rules, art and talent be damned. America did not mind laughing, even at themselves, but the rule was, and is, if it's a black man talking about white folks *to* white folks, it can be true, it can even be slightly insulting, but it damn better well be *funny!*

Attitudes could change drastically where black folks and whites were concerned. A shop-worn joke strikes the absurdity of the black vs white scenario.

During the height of the Battle of Richmond, a Negro in the Union Army shot another black soldier in the Confederate ranks. A Confederate officer who witnessed the shooting turned to a fellow officer and snarled, "Did you see what that nigger *did to our coloured boy?"*

Grier and Cobbs knew the truth, writing that the more a black man "approaches the American ideal of respectability, the more this hostility (the soul of the Bad Nigger) must be repressed."

In 1963 Pryor opened a *Newsweek* magazine and was confronted with the success of the young Bill Cosby. It "fucked me up," claims Pryor. "I said, 'Goddamnit, this nigger's doin' what *I'm* fixin' to do. I want to be the only nigger, ain't no room for two niggers."

Pryor packed and moved to New York, bringing with him a motley array of *niggers* which he was about to introduce to America.

Pryor was nigger to Cool Cos' Negroes. It was a wonder that he expected to succeeed, at least on the terms he had set up to that point. He wasn't speaking the same language! He wasn't coming from the same place.

Here I sit
With my shoes mismated,
Lawdy-mercy!
I's frustrated!
—L. Hughes

Chapter 4: Uppity Nigger!

The sixties were about action. The grease was getting hot and the pot was no longer melting folks down or simmering or smouldering. It was about to sizzle and burn!

Pryor didn't like the atmosphere of Greenwich Village when he stormed the Big Apple in search of his fortune. He felt the people, black and white, were snobs. They probably thought worse of him, unaccustomed as most people are to dealing with genius in its raw and embryonic stages. Pryor had a temper. He was a mean brother when he got a notion to be. But Pryor was a man who was in touch with his times, his place in those times, his people and the streets. They were mean times. How could Pryor be otherwise? He drew his material from the sizzling, burning font, not from the "We shall overcome" group that was marching through the South.

The Village was peopled by the remnants of the Beat Generation, who were still searching through the vapors of their drugs for identity, and a new more ambitious generation, nudging the beats out as they bumped heads in their attempt to drop *into* the system. Pryor was the odd man. But he was too talented to be put out.

Pryor worked the Cafe Wha? when he first hit the Village. He took his act to Poppa Hud's and The Improvisation, getting his act together and talking shit like no other black comedian had ever done, even the notorious Redd Foxx.

Pryor paid a few dues on the circuit that took him through the Catskill resorts where there really *wasn't no niggers* or Negroes. His debut in a small Canadian nightclub ended abruptly one night when he worked opposite a dancing bear which got into the booze and tore the place up.

Pryor tried his act before a Canadian audience of lumberjacks. Another club was wrecked. Whether Pryor's routine was at the center of the trouble is unclear. No one would ever challenge the possibility that it was.

Bill Cosby was the funny man of the hour, his innocent reminiscences funny and universal in a way that was more acceptable.

Flip Wilson was fashioning a strange combination of Cosby and Pryor antics which became parodies of stereotypes which were already in the world of parody—Wilson's version of black minstrels' versions of white black-face minstrels' versions of slaves mocking Master. Many would say that Wilson is more entertainer than artist and social critic, exploiting rather than innovating.

It was through the efforts of Dick Gregory, who probably paved the way for Pryor, the prophet of the seventies, that white people were forced into a pocket where they could not simply laugh at black people. Gregory was forcing them to deal with one very real fact—*Ain't nuthin' funny about being black in America!*

"Isn't this the most fascinating country in the world?" Gregory once asked. "Where else would I ride on the back of the bus, have a choice of going to the worst schools, eating in the worst restaurants, living in the worst neighborhoods, and average $5,000 a week just talking about it?"

Gregory was talking about America. He was Dozens-playing on a more sophisticated plane, but it was the Dozens all the same. And he put his money and time where his mouth was, spending a great deal of time in helping the Civil Rights Movement, marching, picketing, and generally raising hell about the way America was doing things to black folks. Pryor was *going-for* bad. Gregory was *baaaaaad!* They never called him crazy either.

"Greg would rather picket than perform!" close friends observed as Gregory lost job after job due to time spent in jail or marching, or simply the backlash from whites who felt that Gregory had forgotten that he was *supposed to be funny*.

Amos n' Andy had died. And white folks were being placed in a position where they had to start taking Negroes seriously. They were in shock.

Gregory wasn't funny anymore, Cosby was just too cool for a lot of people and Foxx was too raw. What the country needed was a young Negro comedian who could be funny *all the time*. A few insults were perfectly all right.

Pryor seemed to fit the bill. He was young, wiry, had a big mouth, was wild—something that Gregory and Cosby were definitely not—and he wasn't a seemingly political person off the stage. He made people laugh. Of course the people under consideration were white-only.

It was an awkward time for Pryor. He got his first big gigs because of his wild, unbridled genius. White audiences loved to blush and giggle into their handkerchiefs, whispering, "Did he really say *that*? About *us!*?"

Sure he did. And Pryor said more and worse about everyone, anyone. He was an equal opportunity "bad mouther." He'd do the numbers on anybody, including himself.

Here was black humor—or American humor spoke in "ghettoese." Here was black humor that sassed and tickled and teased. Whites could accept it. They only had to see what they wanted—remember Ellison's *Invisible Man*.

Pryor proved out to be the man who could deliver black humor as it was supposed to be delivered. Dramatically. Coldly, Emphatically. Unflinchingly. Relentlessly! As long as he was doing Bill Cosby in bad taste.

It was a bizarre moment in time. The streets were alive with mad rock-, brick- and gun-tottin' black people talkin' some shit that white folks had never heard before, some crazy shit like they, the niggers, were thinking that they could really kick some white ass. People weren't laughing!

Crazy words and phrases, "Get whitey!" "Black Power!" What the hell was going on? Pryor tried to tell them. No one wanted to listen. Everyone wanted to laugh.

58

But Pryor wasn't trying to be simply funny. He was an artist, a complete artist not a dirty joke teller. Of his art Pryor said, "It's like theater. It doesn't matter whether they laugh or not as long as it's interesting and it holds their attention."

It mattered to white audiences. They wanted to laugh first and foremost. If any thinking or soul-searching was to be done, well, they would deal with that later, if ever.

In 1966 Pryor was on his way. He did *On Broadway Tonight* and *Kraft Summer Music Hall,* summer television variety shows. He was good. Pryor said so himself. "I was *very* good."

By 1967 he had done the *Ed Sullivan Show, Merv Griffin* and the *Johnny Carson Show*. That same year Pryor landed a $3,000-a-week gig at a Vegas casino.

Pryor was *good*. Everyone accepted that. But words like "unpredictable," "crazy," "temperamental," "arrogant," and "obnoxious," clouded that excellence. Pryor wouldn't cooperate. He was not playing by rules engraved into the tradition by the Horatio Alger rags to riches tale. Pryor was rich. What business did he have to be nasty, crude, obscene? He had it better than those poor southern blacks, didn't he? The ingrate!

Pryor was in a dilmema. The networks wanted a slightly off-color Cosby. The critics said he was too much like Cosby but the truth was Pryor was gaming himself and everyone else. He was wearing Cosby's jacket but he was still Pryor. And though he made four or five hundred thousand dollars mimicking Cosby he could not clean up himself or his routine enough to be America's best!

"I went to Roy Silver's office," Pryor told David Felton. "Roy Silver used to manage Bill Cosby, and there was this cat who gave me this speech: 'The kind of colored guy we'd like to have over to our house, it's more like Bill Cosby. Now, I'd introduce Bill to my mother, but a guy like you . . .' you know, and I'm *buying* this shit. 'Don't mention the fact that you're a nigger. Don't go into such bad taste.' They were gonna try to help me be nothin' as best they could.''

Richard bought the game. Probably because of the money. And why not? But he tempted the burning in his soul with booze and drugs which unleashed rather than numbed the anger.

That anger bubbled to the surface in 1967 and many of Pryor's problems were due to that anger and his attempts to stifle the painful pangs with drugs and booze.

Cosby's characters were dealing with puberty. Pryor, like his people was trying to survive oppression, alcoholism, drug addiction, racism. They were the same color but didn't come from the same house, while forced to live on the same street.

In early 1967 Pryor got busted for possession of about an ounce of marijuana. In July, Pryor allegedly punched Fabian N. Tholkes, 43, a desk clerk at the Sunset Tower West apartments, and also attacked the owner, Wayne L. Trousper, 34, with a knife and fork.

The actions of an unruly, crude, street person? Overreaction to some mistaken slight? The pressures of success building up? Drugs? Booze? Whatever the cause, Pryor paid $75,000 in an out of court settlement.

Pryor was divorced from his second wife that year and managed to enrage the audience and management of the Aladdin Hotel and Casino in Vegas and was fired for allegedly hurling ''obscenities'' at the audience.

The white audiences—few blacks frequented Vegas at

the time—turned their back on the ungrateful nigger who would not play by the rules. They gave him his chance to be rich and famous and he told them to kiss his ass!

Black people, by and large, were as critical of Pryor, wondering why he was messing up the chance that blacks all over the country were willing to give up their very *soul* for. Was the nigger really crazy? Had the drugs dulled his brain?

"It wasn't me," Pryor said. "I was a robot. *Beep,* Good evening ladies and gentlemen, welcome to the Sands Hotel. Maids here are funny, *Beep."*

Pryor was having his problems with television, too. His reputation for cursing—white people could, blacks couldn't, it wasn't cool—hung over him like a blue-black storm cloud. His moodiness had become legend, and he missed an Ed Sullivan Show appearance because he was "playing" with new camera equipment.

While Pryor was possibly a robot on stage, he certainly wasn't offstage.

"I was a whore then," Pryor said of his early years. But he wasn't for long. Something kept driving him.

"There comes a time in your life," Pryor says, "when the host on the talk show turns to you and says 'Isn't America great, Richard? and you're supposed to say 'It sure is,' and then he says, 'See, guys, *he* did it—what's the matter with the rest of you? I've gone along with that in the past, but no more."

Long before Pryor was born, Paul Robeson, actor/activist/singer/athlete/lawyer/American, balked at the attempts by whites at explaining away the existence of oppression by pointing to his successes. Pryor was not articulating the tenets of rebellion as a Stokely Carmichael might or a Malcolm X might. Pryor was *living* them.

Mel Brooks had this to say of Pryor, though much later in Pryor's life: "His problem is he has many choices, he's rich in choices, and so that inhibits him. Dumber people don't have many choices, so they pursue their goals more easily than Richard does. In order to be free and rich and as emotionally abandoned as Richard is, you have to give up certain safeguards; you risk bananaland, and he risks it every day. He gives himself to each moment in life, totally, without a governor, without a super-ego clocking every moment."

While praising Pryor, Brooks, like most observers, sees many if not all of the misadventures in Pryor's life as due to some "death wish" on Pryor's part, or possibly some mental instability, even genius. "We know that once he settles down," Brooks said, "and he shakes off a couple of, you know, anxious, uh, *emotional traits,* he's just gonna be one of the great(s) . . . ."

What *emotional traits*? What does Brooks mean by "once he settles down?" Should that be read as a suggestion that Pryor shake off some of his *niggerness,* his blackness? Probably. Though Pryor was not allowed to use the term nigger, he was still perceived as such.

The truth is Pryor had very few choices, not because his genius did not allow for a variety of options, but because the system, Black and White, that he was challenging with his genius would not allow him to explore those options.

Pryor's life and work were constantly misread, misinterpreted and redefined by outsiders who refused to recognize other than surface features in a lot of Pryor's work.

Much later Pryor would take the time to explain his position, something he rebelled against doing during his early years in the business. "I was not happy with what I was doing," Pryor said. "And I said, well, this is time to quit; this was my decision. I made a decision about what kind of life I was going to have and I wasn't going to have the kind of life that they were going to give me. People can't give you a life. I wanted to carve mine out!"

The ramblings of a drug addict? A crazed man? A pawn? No way!

"The salient function of (black humor)," says researcher Lawrence Levine, "was to rob the American racial system of any legitimacy long before the courts and the government began that still uncompleted task."

The humorist was not simply an entertainer, he was the watchdog. He kept his sharp eye on everything, peeping it just as it came down, and "told it like it was," with a little *style*. As a bad taste version of Cosby, Pryor wasn't fulfilling this function. While talking about the problems of hotel maids, and telling fairy tales and parodies, his "people" were dying in the streets. He felt that he had sold them out. The reverse was truer. Pryor felt the whore. He wasn't "carving out" his own life.

Even more Pryor's attitude was a slap in the face to the white audiences who "made him wealthy." He was chomping down on the hand that was throwing him the peanuts. What kind of dumb monkey was he? And worse yet, Pryor's freewheeling use of the forbidden word, nigger, was curling more than a few naps among black people who were just getting used to the new suit of clothes they were sportin' as blacks. Negroes were a creation of white folks. They didn't exist.

Pryor's niggers did not fit well in a world peopled by, according to a 1968 *Jet* magazine survey, 37% Afro-

American, 22% Black, 18% Negro, 8% African-American, 5% Colored, 4% American, 6% other assortment of names (nigger wasn't one of them I'm sure). No one understood. Oppression by racism was the only common bond it seemed.

Pryor disregarded the coat-pulling from friends who advised him to clean up his act and get the money and run, and wouldn't listen to the "dichty" Negroes who had decided that they wanted to be called "Afro-American" rather than Negro or black, saying that Pryor's use of the forbidden word would only fuel racism.

No one wanted to call a spade a spade, opting for calling it a shovel or dirt moving utensil, which somehow never changed function or attitude toward that function, real or fancied.

Pryor could not ignore what was before him. It was part and parcel of his genius. Brooks remarked, "He just reports terribly accurately and does not stretch. When he does a junkie or he does a drunk, he does 'em fuckin' right on; I mean, that's it. He gets all the nuances; he gets the breathing right. You say, 'I know that guy, that's true.' And that's blindingly brilliant and amazing."

Writer James McPherson said, "Because he must look (at the world), and because his imagination is essentially comic, he arranges what he sees, no matter how horrible, into comic patterns."

If Pryor is strolling along and a truck load of shit has been dropped into the street, stinking in the noon sun and blocking his path, that's what he's going to deal with—the stinking presence, just as it is. Pryor is not about to go through a series of changes searching for an acceptable way of identifying the problem. He will not say there is a little *poo-poo* in the roadway. That's not the problem. The problem is that there is an entire truck load of stinking shit blocking his way and it's got to be moved. Period!

Pryor's art establishes that there is a very real and raw condition that is going on right now. He's not talking about something he heard somebody say, or about something that somebody else said was said. Pryor is talking about the things that he knows to be be true, from his own experience. And he cherishes even the worst of those moments because they are his. His artistic nature refuses to allow anyone else to define those experiences out of context.

It is this attitude which probably keeps Pryor from talking about his "real stuff." He probably does not trust outsiders with that "very, very special" information. And his audiences were made up of just that, outsiders, the enemy.

All Pryor wanted was for people to laugh, be entertained, enjoy themselves. If there was a catch, it came in that Pryor also hoped that they would really look, listen and see what was going on, what he was trying to put down. He wanted them to move. Stop the flow of shit. Immediately.

But that didn't happen. Malcolm got blown away. Dr. Martin Luther King, Jr., met the same fate. Civil rights workers disappeared. And city streets were turned to "charcoal alleys." Any artist who was plugged into his people and the times would have felt the pressure. Pryor did.

His characters, Pryor's niggers, wanted to be heard, begged to be heard. Vegas didn't want to hear from them. Television couldn't stand the naked truth, and the black people who had the bread to catch a Pryor show, certainly didn't want to be reminded that they existed.

Pryor's niggers weren't just crude, uneducated or unemployed. For too many they represented America's failures. Though they often didn't see themselves that way, they sure wanted to tell somebody, anybody, everybody just how they felt about things.

Vegas said no. Pryor tried to silence the angry throng that bellowed in his brain, sliced at his gut. He numbed himself with booze and charged himself with drugs.

Cocaine, the drug of the wealthy—a white man's drug—became a nigger's trademark. Pryor wore the badge unashamedly. He loved the glistening powder. So did his audience but they would never admit to it. That was part of the Pryor charm, a charm that all blacks had throughout history. He worked well as a scapegoat. No matter how much coke one snorted, Pryor was worse. *Thank God for the nigger*! But not on the stage pointing damning, obnoxious fingers at his betters.

Pryor forced people to face things. He forced Barbara Walters to say "The Word" on national television. "You say that very well," Pryor told her, setting her up for, "You've said it before, haven't you?"

But he also told Walters how much he loved drugs. Was Pryor loaded? Is that why his whole life seemed loaded with potholes?

What about the routine about the "New Niggers" being brought in from Vietnam? Is Pryor spaced out when he suggests that these "New Niggers" will be taught to hate the "Original Nigger?" Is Pryor tripping when he suggests that they will be taught to say *nigger*, convincingly? "If you get your ass whupped, you know you got it!" which ends the playlet, shows that Pryor, while he might be loaded, still knows exactly what he is doing with his art.

Those who would focus on the insanities would push

aside the causes for the insanities. They would look at the blood rushing from a wound and blame the wound, rather than the one who inflicted it.

No matter what his critics might say, Pryor is the first to admit when he is wrong. And more often than not his escapades become meat for his act.

"I snorted cocaine for about fifteen years," Pryor say, then pauses dramatically and adds, "with my *dumb* ass! I musta snorted up Peru. I could of bought Peru, all the stuff I snorted. Could of gave them the money up front and had me a piece of prop'ty."

Some would say Pryor is self-destructive because he flaunts his mistakes. Others expect it of him for some unknown reason. For Pryor it is probably a cathartic experience that he is willing to share with others. Or, just maybe, Pryor knows that his wrong is really not all that serious in comparison to the larger ills of the society.

"I've never hurt anybody in all the bullshit I do," Pryor has said. "In all my dealings those are not my intentions. But it seems to those looking on from the outside that maybe you've hurt yourself.

"Maybe I could hurt myself," Pryor added, "if I'm not aware of what I do. My biggest problem was drinking and snorting cocaine. There was a time when I could do it and have a lot of fun. But I no longer have fun with it and I don't want to self-destruct myself."

But Pryor did self-destruct. All will agree that it was an unavoidable, or at least a predictable event, given the lifestyle that Pryor had taken on during that period David Felton would like to call Pryor's "Super Nigger" period. But it would not be altogether true.

It is too easy to point to Pryor's excesses as being at the root of his so-called "madness" without glancing at the possible causes of the excesses. But the easy way is the American way, and the public would only accept that Pryor just could not handle his genius, the big money and the big time.

He just wasn't a professional. The same flack came from the Negro camp.

More to the point Pryor's temporary split from active participation in his own degradation was due to a combination of things. Many of those things were responsible for the madness that had killed Dr. Martin Luther King, Jr., in the early months of 1968; the slaughter that was steadily growing in Southeast Asia; the murder of Malcolm X; an all-out conspiracy formulated by the law enforcement body of this nation directed at those people who were about change; and reactions to those things. The times had become explosive.

While Pryor had managed to cop a role as a fumbling detective in a Sid Caesar film, *Busy Body* (1966), his people, the unwashed street folk, were being offed by policemen. Pryor, though brilliant in the role, was not relating to the very people he cared most about. They were gnawing at his guts, Mudbone, 300 pound Big Bertha and her 280 pound ass; Jesse, Oilwell, all of them. They had something to say and no one was providing them with a medium through which they could say it. And they didn't plan on being delicate about the way they said what they had to say.

"Sometimes I get so mad," said Pryor on the *Tonight* Show (1968). "I feel like getting undressed and running across the (Vegas) tables shouting 'Black Jack! Black Jack!'"

Reality has blended with fantasy over the years and Pryor's streak across the gaming tables is allegedly something that really took place.

Pryor would say much later, "You know the casino, the gambling routine, the finish. I didn't feel good. I didn't feel I could tell anybody to kiss my ass, 'cause I didn't have no ass, you dig? My ass was on my face."

In the streets you've got to be able to *bring ass to get ass*! Pryor went to war and didn't bring ass, or at least give it up before the fight got started good. He was trying to win a battle using weapons the enemy laid on him. Weapons that frustrated the user, fucked with his mind.

Felton wrote that Pryor "claims it was his professional life that was getting him down—his material, the pressures on him to keep it as clean and anonymous as casino money, and the realization that ultimately he would never be successful, that as a Cosby imitator he would always be the opening act for someone else."

But Felton would qualify his remarks by writing, "From 1967 through at least 1970, he underwent what might be called his Super Nigger period." Felton sees the period as "a time when, perhaps, financial success went to his head, or more specifically, to his nose. Richard admitted that he was then heavily into cocaine." Again the drug fixation which really only complicated the real problem, the world's inability to adapt to a very real presence in the form of Pryor's niggers asserting themselves.

Critics will point to Pryor's 1974 indictment for failing to pay taxes on a robust $250,000 earned during his super nigger period. Pryor was fined $2500 and jailed for ten days. The real problem was simply that Pryor was out of his class, he couldn't take care of business.

There was no doubt that Pryor wasn't taking care of business. He admitted as much. But business wasn't his forte. Pryor was an artist, a poet, a genius. Was he expected to excel in business too? Of course! Especially if he was to become the number one Negro in the country, edging Cosby out of the limelight. Pryor was expected to prove that America worked for even the less polished of its Negroes. Pryor accepted that role, for a minute.

"I'd changed my mind about what I wanted to do. I was involved in leading a new life and that old shit didn't matter."

What new life? What old shit?

According to Felton the new life began in 1969 when Pryor shed the Cosby routine and presented his characters to an audience that was not prepared for what was happening. Hell, they were still wondering why the colored populace of the country was raising so much hell. America was one helluva lot better than Russia, or Vietnam or even Africa. What did they want? What did Richard Pryor want?

Pryor was running across the country screaming "Black Jack! Black Jack! Black Jack!" It was an act of rebellion from Pryor's Nigger Handbook. He wasn't being the kind of black that white people wanted to invite into their homes. He wasn't cute!

McPherson wrote, "Pryor's people are real and immediately recognizable by anyone who has had contact with them, whether in a black skin or a white one. He does not allow them to get away with anything. Pryor is giving a public airing to some of the more unadmirable styles of the urban black community and making his audiences recognize them for what they are . . . it is Pryor's genius to be able to make his audiences aware that the characters, though comic, are nonetheless complex human beings."

Recognizable or not, complex human beings or no, America wanted no part of them. "When I didn't do characters," Pryor said, "white folks liked me."

70

Why did he force these people on his audience? Didn't he know that the real beauty in black humor was it's ability to protect and shield the jokester who has just pulled a fast one on Master? Master would laugh and everything would be fine.

Here's an example of an old slave joke that reflects the wilyness that kept slaves alive: a slave got caught after eating one of master's prized pigs. In defense of his "wrong-doing" the slave offers: "Yes, suh, Massa, you got less pig now but you sho' got more nigger."

Unfortunately for Pryor, white folks of the sixties were sick and tired of niggers. They wanted more pig. Pryor wasn't about to back away from issuing large doses of nigger whenever he got the chance. The chances were coming farther and farther apart.

In 1968 a Chicago columnist reported that Pryor had been banned from future appearances on the *Joey Bishop Show* because of his alleged too-liberal use of profanity while doing a week-long stint on the show.

Producer Paul Orr denied that Pryor was banned, and said, "He didn't use any profanity on the Joey Bishop Show. We're going to use him again."

Pryor was scheduled for an appearance for the third week in June of that year. The Bleep Brigade was readied for action.

What was the matter with Pryor? Is what Felton suggested true? Was Pryor simply feeling like a Super Nigger? Did he think that his stuff was so good that he didn't have to tone it down to fit his audience? Had the drugs befuddled him? Or was it something quite different?

"I think there's a thin line between being a Tom on them people (source of his characters)," said Pryor, "and seeing them as human beings. When I do the

71

people, I have to do it true. If I can't do it, I'll stop right in the middle rather than pervert it and turn it into Tomism. There's a thin line between to laugh *with* and to laugh *at*."

All that was well and good, but why didn't Pryor play the game? All black folks know how to play the man for whatever they can get.

Bledsoe, principal of a black institution in Ellison's *Invisible Man*, in acknowledging that he plays a game with the school's white benefactors explains, "Why the dumbest black bastard in the cotton patch knows that the only way to please a white man is to tell a lie!"

"I know all the tricks," Pryor said to an interviewer. "I assume that everybody does."

Why didn't he use them? Why didn't he wear the mask? Take the shit? The money was good! And wasn't part of the game to please white folks so that they would shower down their good graces in the form of money and favors?

Pryor knew the game. He joked his way out of a Philadelphia jail in 1967. Accused of assault, Pryor did his number on the judge who was moved to say: "Anybody's got as much talent as you don't belong in jail. Case dismissed."

"The joke," wrote Freud, "represents a rebellion against . . . authority, a liberation from pressures."

Maybe Pryor was about the business of liberation. Maybe Pryor had decided that it was no longer necessary for blacks to alter themselves, their attitudes, their rhythms, their language to please white people. Maybe, at the same time, he was trying to warn white people of the dangers inherent in the absurd practices that racism sponsors. Maybe Pryor really found that to compete with Bill Cosby was to deny the existence of either of their worlds and the characters in them and accept some perverted images which would please whites.

"I don't know what I do," Pryor says. "I know what I *won't* do. I don't know what I will do. I turned down big money because I won't work Vegas and be that type."

The "type" Pryor speaks of is an alien creation of an unsympathetic audience. Pryor, like any artist, was simply refusing to paint with someone else's brush and colors, in their style.

"I love what I do very much," Pryor said of his work. "It's the only thing in my life that's never hurt me, that's given me fulfillment, and let me have my dignity. Never belittled me."

"I'm black and I'm proud!" was the battle cry of the late sixties. It was the battle cry that would usher in the end of a great movement as it was the one cry that white America was not prepared to confront. "I'm black and I'm proud!" was not simply a reactionary phrase, a weak counterpunch of rhetoric directed at the might of the clenched fist of racism. It was an imperative. An affirmation! It was a mighty "Kiss my ass!" to all things white, which had heretofore been flaunted as what was happening.

White America approached what it considered a "problem" originating in the ranks of black folks rather than their own in the same manner it approached the "Indian Problem." With force, trickery and even murder.

Pryor was caught up in the same frenzy. He had to be. He was still a street nigger though he could snort coke with the richest of the white folks. Richard Pryor wasn't acceptable baggage. He had to conform.

73

Pryor didn't conform. And because he didn't or couldn't conform Pryor was forced to raise the question, "What the fuck am I doing here?"

In typical Pryor style, he waited until he was standing before a packed crowd in the Alladin Hotel. He made his decision to chuck it all, or went "crazy" as many believe or suffered a form of "nervous breakdown" as Pryor would have us believe. Whatever the case, Pryor stormed off in the wrong direction, also typical of the events surrounding his life, and found the space at the wrong end of the stage was "supposedly" too small for him to use as an exit. "The panel at that end," Pryor said later, "was like two times smaller than I was, and the guy's saying, 'No, you can't go through there.' And I'm saying, 'Yeah, I can' . . . and I squeezed through . . . 'cause I wasn't going back across the stage."

Pryor was 30 years old and making six thousand dollars a week at the posh Vegas gambling joint by simply doing a few shows of fairy tale parodies, army jokes, and talk show routines. Easy enough labor for that kind of bread. It almost killed Pryor to give up the bread. But when he raised the question, he answered it with a solid, "Fuck it!"

I laid down last night
Turnin' from side to side
I was not sick, Lawd
Just disstisfied.

5

Chapter 5: Up With Nigger!

Berkeley, California, is a sleepy little bedroom community in the Bay area of Northern California. Most
probably, had it not been for the University of California located there, Berkeley would have been doomed
to the same anonymity as Peoria, Illinois, without
Richard Pryor.

Richard Pryor, "What the fuck am I doing here?"
still fresh on his lips, his eyes wide and curious, questioning, slipped into the quiet little community and
pulled the covers over his head so that he could block
out the shit and think.

Think about what? Most felt that what Richard Pryor
really needed was some couch time with a head doctor.
Pryor later said that he had suffered a "sort of nervous
breakdown" that night on the stage of the Aladdin

hotel. But why? The bread was good. Maybe too good, some say. What more could he want? What more could anybody want? He was on his way to becoming HNIC (Head Nigger In Charge) of black comedy in America. He was rich. He had access to television. What did Pryor want?

Pryor wanted to escape, for one. There is no doubt he felt trapped by the restrictions forced on him. He said it, "Bleep, I felt like a robot! *Bleep*!"

Robot? If so, one of the highest paid mechanical contraptions in the history of the world. Why wasn't he satisfied? Why couldn't he cool down? People loved him when he was not *sooo* black and unfunny. "He can be a very funny man," said Johnny Carson in a *Rolling Stone* interview. "I'd like to see him not be so dirty," Carson added, " 'cause I don't think he needs it."

That was part of what Pryor had to investigate. He was charged with being dirty. He was constantly indicted and condemned for being racist. Serious charges which could burden a sensitive man. Pryor is sensitive, possibly to the point of eccentricity. Even though he had found within himself the ability—which is a dubious quality at times—to say "fuck it!", it is something he worries about because he is sensitive to how he is perceived by others. He does not like to be misread.

Pryor escaped. And though he is, by his own admission, not the academic sort, Pryor found that he needed to place his life in the proper context. Things were happening too fast. He had to organize the chaos that racked his mind or succumb to a very real insanity. Possibly the kind that destroyed Lenny Bruce and Freddie Prinz.

Away from the clamor of the bright lights of Vegas Pryor could more readily investigate the energies and urges that sizzled in his soul. He was evolving. He was raising questions that he had only skirted before, numbing them, as he did himself with his favorite lady.

Was he really all that violent? Was he anti-social? Was he self-destructive?

"I was a whore," Pryor admits later. And by that he meant that he had sold himself out. That he had gone for the bread and forgotten the voices and faces in his brain which begged for a chance to be seen and heard. It was an enlightening admission. It cleared away some of the debris that clogged his brain. But there was much more to do. He had responsibilities. His fourth child, Rain, was born in 1970.

Snug in the Berkeley community Pryor kicked back and "got naked" and "just sat in (his) house and didn't come out until (he) was ready."

Was Pryor simply tired? Was he hibernating or hiding? Could he live without the big bucks? The audiences? The applause? The bright lights? The fabulous hotel suites?

"That was the most exciting time," Pryor told David Felton. "'Cause I got an apartment, $110 a month, and it was mine, and every fucking piece of furniture in there was mine; I bought it. I didn't have nobody in that house I didn't like, you know what I mean? Didn't no motherfucker come near I didn't want there."

These are the words of a man rebelling against more than just his gig. Pryor was at odds with more than just the Alladin Hotel and television. It was a great possibility that there was a small group of "hangers-on" trailing after him snorting up his leavings and bad-mouthing him on top of everything.

But why Berkeley? Why not the Bahamas? Jamaica? Africa? Hollywood? Was it because of the sizzling reputation that surrounded the small college town? Some say the easy access to cocaine lured Pryor to Berkeley.

Pryor read Malcolm and grooved to Marvin Gaye's album "What's Going On?" He was confronting his supposed "crazy" side with the heaviest guns he could find.

Most critics and a few fans had written Pryor off as too hard to handle. He had blown too many chances. He had upset too many people with his "niggerish" antics. Very few people get anywhere close to the top of the heap. And no one, even white folks, makes it twice.

And what did a wild, coke-snorting, violent, unpredictable dude like Pryor have going for him? Cosby made it through college. "If I didn't make good at Temple University," Cos recalled, "I knew what waited for me was a lifetime as a busboy or a factory hand. I was so afraid that I made myself do well."

Pryor didn't go to college, at least in the classical sense of going to college. San Jose State College gave him a Ph.D. in Black Street History. Pryor know how to *survive*. It's something one learns early in the streets. Still, there's little marketability beyond the streets where the real money is. Or was Pryor after something quite different? Maybe that's what he meant when he said, "I changed my mind about what I wanted to do." Maybe the big bucks didn't mean anything to him anymore. Maybe he really wasn't crazy at all, just dancing to the beat of a different drummer, keeping time to Marvin Gaye's "What's Going On?" If Pryor meant it when he said, "I am what I do," then there's no doubt that he had to find out what was going on or really go crazy.

But it would seem that a sane man would pick a much better time in life to question motivation, direction,

80

being. Pryor could go no higher. He had been a television regular, exchanging snappy repartee with America's greatest talk show hosts, and had completed no less than two movie parts. A black comedian could ask for no more from America.

It is probably because there was really nothing left for him to strive for that made Pryor balk at what he was doing. At his worst he was too good for the audiences that came to see him. And he knew it, after he got his head together. Something happened to Pryor. It was the artist taking control.

"I did TV regularly," Pryor said later, "Mike Douglas, Carson. But I don't want to do that shit no more. I don't want to get involved with those people—their ideas and views are not mine. I was doing their humor and being judged by them. 'Was he good enough? Can he come back? Did they like him out there in middle-America' and that shit? . . . but there was a whole other kind of artist coming out in me. I went to work for people who could relate to me—after-hours spots, a few little nightclubs here and there, colleges, stuff like that. I got my act in shape and now I'm going back to TV on my own terms. I signed my own ticket."

Maybe he didn't run to Berkely just because he could get close to the magic powder that supposedly kept him going. Maybe the electric atmosphere that rocketed the University of California at Berkeley into national prominence had somethng to do with it. Maybe Pryor was looking for room to stretch out. He went home so to speak, back to the streets where it all started. Isn't that the only place where he was really appreciated?

Pryor, like many other black people in America, was probably facing one of the most severe identity crises he would ever face. And Pryor's "I am what I do!" became his own revolutionary cry which meshed with the dying cries of "I'm black and I'm proud!" and "Black Power!" which were losing in the battle against racism.

"You don't have to do what you don't want to do," explained Pryor of his so-called unpredictability, based on his continued refusal to bow to the whims of audiences and noncreative people who do not know, and generally do not care, where he is coming from.

"You have to make your stand. Ya gotta say, 'I ain't gonna do this shit no more' just the way I did. You gotta find an alternative. As long as you look for something, nature will show you where it is at. The gods won't forsake you. All of life is like a treasure, if you get your head where you can deal with it. I control my energy, but I can feel nature and luck helping me out."

Was Pryor loaded when he put that bit of philosophy together? What gods? Is it just more jive from the King of Jive? No! Pryor, like a great many blacks, had made a decision, and that decision revolved around rejecting resigned acceptance of what or who they were and taking charge of who they were and how they would be perceived. It was simply a taking charge of one's own thing, and damn the consequences. "Fuck it!" writ large and articulate.

"I love being black and love being who I am," Pryor said. "And I'm happy for all the success I have and the fact that it is coming from black people. I'm doing what I do, making money from my people, and I feel good, man, trying to do my shit."

Maybe that's the key to the Pryor mystery. The man had decided, with or without the help of drugs and booze, that he just wasn't going to take the shit anymore. He, like Malcolm X who had been wasted years before, knew that there was no other way that a man could live his life. Pryor was going to be that kind of man. And maybe he was damn scared about making the decision. Throwing away six thousand a week would make anyone's knees weak. And how could he know that black people would still buy his product, pay to come see him?

It didn't matter. Pryor was listening to Gaye and digging Malcolm and his mind was clicking into place. The stuff that Malcolm had put down was not for the faint of heart, the turn coat, the compromiser. "I think," said Malcolm, his face set hard, intense, "that white people in this country should be made to realize that if something isn't done to bring an immediate halt to the oppression and brutality that is being inflicted upon Negroes, then the Negro should be considered justified in doing whatever is necessary to protect himself. That means WHATEVER is necessary to protect himself. He shouldn't initiate any aggressive action, but he is within his rights—self-defense is dependable in any court of law."

An historic picture shows Malcolm X, automatic rifle in hand, peering from the window of his home. He and his family lived constantly under the threat of death. Malcolm was wasted for what he was putting down. Pryor stepped out of the limelight and into that world where he pulled some of the strings.

In 1971 Pryor cut his second album, 'Craps' *After Hours*, for Laff records. Warner/Reprise produced his first album, *Richard Pryor*. Recorded live at the Redd Foxx Club in Hollywood, 'Craps' *After Hours* is significant in that it reflects the impact that Malcolm had on Pryor which would help to put down any suggestion that Pryor was simply afraid of the big time, of competing with white folks on their own turf.

Pryor was not hiding out in the small nightclubs and dives where he performed "for people who could relate." He was finally taking care of business, at least with regard to his art. He was developing his own thing and that thing was going to be something that he would take to the world, on his own terms. That was Malcolm's way.

And Pryor listened because he and Malcolm X, one-time criminal Malcolm Little, came from the same kind of streets. They spoke the same language, one that Malcolm spoke loud and proud until he was assassinated.

Pryor didn't have to relearn the language. He had never really moved that far from it. He only had to refine the nuances, check out the new rhythms that were flowing in the streets, and get a perspective on the whole thing. He was talking nigger shit louder than before. He had to be right, because there weren't a great many people around who were going to pay just to hear what niggers had to say.

The '*Craps*' *After Hours* album told it like it was in the very real language of the streets. It was hard, some say too hard; it was biting, often bitter. But it was very, very real and that was exactly what Pryor wanted to be putting down.

Malcolm X said: "Any time I have a religion that won't let me fight for my people, I say to hell with that religion."

Pryor said: "Religion fucked a lot of people up . . . Go to church with no money and don't you feel bad . . . Put something in the collection plate? Kiss my ass! Put some shit in it. You giving shit. Here's some more!"

Malcolm X said: "White man, call yourself a hate teacher because you invented hate. Call yourself a racist because you invented the race problem."

84

Pryor: "White folks don't give a nigger a break. Jackson Five be singing their asses off and they be talking about the Osmond Brothers. Fuck the Osmond Brothers!"

Later Pryor would say to an interviewer, "Niggers got to go to school out of self-defense. You can't afford to be ignorant. It is their world and we are living in it. This ain't our language, so this society is not ours and we are not a part of it. But we got to go to college so we can become all this shit. Just to get it back to where it is . . . We need minds to deal with the trickery."

Is Pryor paraphrasing Malcolm's "Education is our passport to the future, for tomorrow belongs to the people who prepare for it today."

"The answer is war," Pryor said, "a heavy black and white war, people against people, poor people against greedy people . . . There's a box of greedy people controlling what we do."

And Malcolm said, "You get your freedom by letting your enemy know that you'll do anything to get your freedom; then you'll get it."

Maybe it was Malcolm who gave organization to the chaos that was Pryor's life up to that time. Malcolm couldn't give Pryor all the answers because Malcolm didn't have them. But it was Malcolm who let Pryor know that there were others who thought like he did. Malcolm helped Pryor realize that he wasn't really crazy, at least not the kind of crazy that would make him a prime package for the nut house.

Pryor was crazy like Malcolm was crazy. Crazy enough to stand up and say "fuck it!" knowing that there was a lot more ass out there to whup than one man could handle.

But it was 1971 and the mood of the country had

changed, or at least the mood that the country was in. Little else changed. Attitudes were the same, though on the surface it seemed that much was happening. Most of the big bad militants had been chased out of the country, wasted, jailed or found to be working for the man, on the quiet side. A few blacks had gotten a few well-paying very visible gigs, and it seemed that the revolution wouldn't be really necessary after all. At least that was the tune that was being played over and over. Some thought it had come and gone.

The change of tempo helped Pryor, though unintentionally. Black folks had been discovered by the motion picture industry but not the good, too-much-like-the-white-folks-black-folks. The industry had dredged up that loud talking, don't take no shit from no jive motherfucker-nigger. The whitey haters! The discovery meant big money for the discoverers who found that there was a wide audience of pseudo-revolutionaries who would not take to the streets behind Malcolm but who would munch-a-bunch while cheering *Shaft, The Legend of Nigger Charley, Sweetback's Baaaadassss Song, Super Fly* and the rest.

The industry had allowed that there were a few bad, meaning not good, i.e., nasty, racist, white folks out there in the real world and they selectively brought them to the silver screen. There, with all the style and effort of home movies, they fed these ne'er do wells to the angry blacks who were looking for fresh white meat. It worked!

Some black folks screamed out that the films were racist and exploitive. Black actors defended themselves and the films, saying that they weren't exploitive; or that maybe some of them were but they weren't really racist. Just good clean fun. At least blacks, unlike the

Indians, were beating white folks, albeit the white folks were the most despicable kind that could be found—larcenous, overweight, oversexed lawmen from the rural South, big bad gangsters from the North, dope pushers, distortions all. Somehow there really were no bad guys, at least no white ones, preaching racism in the churches and in the banks and in the front offices of motion picture companies.

Everyone was saying "nigger." At least in the movies. Black folks were swaggering in the streets, though the marching soon stopped. There was no one to follow. Black folks swaggered alone, like big bad *Shaft*, and *Super Fly*. This was the beginning of the "Super Nigger Period." It was similar to Pryor's Super Nigger Period only in that all the images were restricted from without. Blacks were working in the industry. They were on the big screen. And though they said The Word loud and often, the nuances were gone, it wasn't the same language, it didn't mean the same thing. Whites were restricting any real efforts at true creation.

Filmmaker Gordon Parks, Jr., who directed *Super Fly* said, "Any film that doesn't go into any depth in the characterization of what those people are, is obviously made in a way to rip-off people. It uses all those cliche things in life to draw people in to see it."

Black people were seriously concerned about image. Down with stereotypes was the cry! But the films kept rolling out developed by white writers and producers for black actors. The age of minstrelsy had returned, or rather resurfaced where it could be seen and heard in full color. Maybe black people really weren't that concerned. At least not as concerned as Pryor was. He found the guts, or was crazy enough to say fuck it!

There were blacks who really believed that they had

"overcome," citing that the only problem facing the black race in America was of its own making. Pryor was still name-calling and pointing damning fingers at white people. What was he doing, trying to stir up more trouble? Hadn't there been enough killing and burning and hate talk? He was part of the problem to some blacks.

Pryor didn't think so. And there were others who felt the same. The young people picked up what he was putting down and it didn't sound anything like, "Hey, white folks, let me have the chance to be what you want me to be." Pryor was saying, "Look, motherfucker. You best to take me like I am because you've had a whole lot to do with my being this way. You dig!"

While the black exploitation flicks were adding more bullshit to the already steaming piles of stereotypes from which white folks drew their images of blacks, Pryor was creating, dabbing his brush into the rich colors of the streets he knew and bringing those streets to life just as they were, with an added twist provided by the Pryor genius.

The ones who did not listen did not understand. They were about other things. Change, yes, but methods differed greatly. The gates were opening and the "Me" generation was about to be cut loose on the world.

Pryor still fit in. His rebellious nature, his flippancy, blasphemous routines, all made Pryor attractive to an audience that was desperately trying to cut itself off from all tradition that would stop them from enjoying life. And crazy as Pryor was, he did know how to sniff out the most in life.

White folks were trying to straighten out some of the chaos that sprang up in the sixties. The movies helped. Blacks weren't mad at all white people. Malcolm and the Black Muslims and all blacks who said *all* whites were racist, were racists themselves. The movies pointed to the bad whites, and that was that. If a nigger talked bad about any other white, *he* would prove himself to be the racist.

"The things I have to do in order to be on (TV)," said Pryor, "just destroy me too much. It's really weird, like they make me feel like thanking them for letting me degrade myself. So I try not to do it."

Pryor backed off and the others scrambled for the slot left open. Slowly, even cautiously, "ethnic television" evolved out of the crap left over after everyone finally discovered that as bad as he was Supper Nigger just "couldn't fly."

The Super Nigger fare had taken the punch out of Pryor's imperative. The Super Nigger was quickly moved beyond the level of reality, where a revolutionary hero could function, to the level of fantasy. That kind of shit just didn't happen in the for real streets, and everybody knew it! Some thought it was cool. Cathartic even. A slap in whitey's face. " *'Bout time the movies showed some niggers gettin' over on white folks*!"

"You take a black guy who has to take a lot of bull all day," said Bill Cosby in 1972, "working in a car wash. He goes to see *Shaft* or *Buck and The Preacher* and he gets a certain release out of it."

Release? Is that what those celluloid comic books were about? Laxatives for all the bottled up misery in the black folks who flocked to see them? Did they pass out toilet paper before and during the showings?

They might as well have for all the good many of them did. While a great many actors would justify their participation in the exploitive process as at least giving jobs to black people and allowing a positive image to be shown, Bill Cosby hit closer to home when he said, "It's a color scheme that's being played out in a lot of these black films. It's called back-atcha. In *The French Connection*, you had a white cop come into a black junkies' bar and treat them all like dirt. In *Shaft's Big Score*, you have a black cop do the same thing in a white bar."

Unfortunately the films that showed whites getting over were closer to reality. Black films were nothing more or less than dangerous forms of escapism when blacks should have been controlling images rather than attacking the false ones many blacks helped to create.

Unlike Pryor's Oilwell who boasts to the police, "I'm Oilweeeeelll. I'm 422 pounds of maa*aaaan*!" and gets his ass beat, Shaft is a figment. Oilwell lives and dies in the streets. His blood is real. He cannot fly. Super Fly is only "Fly" in the dark confines of a motion picture house. Shaft swaggered. He had no program, real or fancied. It was like jumping off of a garage with a sheet for a cape. A serious fall was pending.

Pryor never let his people stray from the possibilities and liabilities that gave them life, that burdened them, that sometimes killed them. Opposite Pryor the burgeoning crop of so-called black films were nothing more or less than white "fairytales," with none of the interest and color of those supposedly compiled by Joel Chandler Harris—Uncle Remus and Company.

Redd Foxx, the blue comic, once bragged, "When I first started doing dirty jokes, everybody told me if I cleaned up, I'd be famous. I didn't clean up, but I got famous anyway." Foxx traded in his blue cloud for a battered pair of boots and a junk yard and emerged as the Sanford half of *Sanford and Son*. It was a hit. And why not. Wasn't it spun off from reality? It worked when it was *Steptoe and Son* in England. There was no reason why it couldn't work in "blackface" in America.

It was the kind of tongue in cheek humor that America was ready to accept. America wanted to laugh, not think, at least not those who accounted for television ratings. Good clean one-liners that poked fun at obvious racists and buffons on either side of the color coin was the vogue. It was something the industry was sure would please everyone. And Foxx carried The Word with him to his new successful show.

The world was suspicious of Mudbone but they loved Foxx's Sanford, a blustering, dozen-playing, harmless old goat. Sanford would never lead a revolution. A drunk Mudbone might do anything.

Pryor came out of hiding in 1972, dragging his tattered reputation with him. There was no doubt that he was good at what he did. Everyone agreed on that. There was a great deal of uncertainty as to how to get him to do what he did best without his "going off." And then there was the problem of censoring him for television. The Word was okay, Pryor just took loose language to the extreme. Television audiences, especially middle-America, weren't ready for any number of "motherfuckers" even said in jest. America didn't think that kind of stuff was funny.

The "sitcom" was a boon and a bust. Blacks worked and every now and then one of them was funny. Pryor wrote a few scripts for *Sanford and Son* and for Flip Wilson. It was a new trip for Pryor. The film industry provided the arena where his characters might stretch out a little more, flesh out in shape, form, color, costume, context. And it was needed!

Middle-America, through shabbily written and shallow sitcoms, was getting a wrong impression of its role in the development of America and the roles played by the other people who helped to make up the American political and social body. Pryor's work provided that yardstick by which one could judge what was really happening in the world, a world distorted by "sitcom" robots who spout endless reams of one-liners and the choking flood of Super Nigger films which only frustrate rather than educate or entertain.

Pryor had spent his two years, 1970-1972, putting his whole program together, testing himself and his characters before excited audiences at Mandrake's in Berkeley and Basin St. West in San Francisco. Was he ready?

When Pryor emerged from his self-imposed hibernation he brought a crowd with him. An angry crowd of niggers that dispelled all the cuteness that would become popular in "sitcoms" which, though about blacks in America, were directed at whites in middle-America. Each "ethnic show" was dutifully altered, reshaped, sapped of all worth, according to the dictates of an alien audience that television is somehow afraid to offend, they say, with the truth.

Even worse, it was found by those few who took the time to really take a look at things, that there was a peculiar characteristic about the white American public, a protective device insulated them from the truth—especially if it didn't fit their prejudices.

"I am an invisible man . . . " says Ellison's *Invisible Man*, ". . . simply because people (whites) refuse to see me . . . When they approach me they see only my surroundings, themselves, or figments of their imagination—indeed, everything and anything except me."

The ethnic lineup had swollen from *Sanford and Son* to the weak *That's My Mama, Good Times* and *Chico and the Man*—an East L.A. version of *Sanford and Son*.

It looked as if television was finally paying long over-due tribute to the common man, the little man who really made America click. The unemployed and the "most shuffling, sly, stupid, cunning, dishonest, ridiculous buffoon to play a continuing character on television," as Wall Street Journal critic Benjamin Stein described the affable Sanford as played by Redd Foxx.

One can argue that the character was misread by the critic because he really didn't understand what was happening. The nuances kept him from really getting into the character.

That would be a hip argument if all the shows had been written by Pryor, or some other street writer, in the vernacular of the street. Stein was fairly close to being right, even though Foxx did his best to keep the show on a level where it wasn't insulting. The show, like most of the junk on television, was superficial. It caught the color of the clothes and some of the motions of the dance but missed the rhythm that drove the whole thing.

Sanford's drunk in-law, Woody, is a pathetic drunk. He has no "knowledge." "You take some 63-year-old cat on the street," Pryor said, "ugly, spit coming out his mouth—he's still got something you can't have. You can't say he didn't see that gutter or he didn't drink this wine. That's the knowledge."

Knowledge, soul, essence, all interchangeable in this regard, cannot be mimicked, copied or captured if it is not understood. No one ever tried. Where was the need?

Pryor's drunks had a pathetic side, too. They could not be glorified. They weren't saints, saviors, or heroes. But they survived a helluva lot more than a great many who have risen to those particular positions in the national mind. Pryor let them keep their dignity while confessing their faults.

When the wino tries to help the young junkie by pulling the youngster's coat to his shortcomings, he cannot help but admit to his own weaknesses, something Pryor refuses to hide or let his people hide. It gives them their human quality. It makes what they say worth hearing. It is a quality which gives Pryor's niggers value where none can be found in the many "blaxploitation flicks" that claimed to be "right on" with the black experience and the *real* black man who could fuck and fight his ass off but somehow just couldn't get the "cotton" of his breath or the boot out of his ass. And while there were those who saw little difference between Pryor's people and the larger-than-life brigade, there indeed was a difference which accounts for the quick demise of the blaxploitation flick and Pryor's longevity.

The so-called bourgeois Negro had become villain, as all monied people are so labeled when the film industry attempts to celebrate the common man who generally turns out to be nothing more or less than noble savage or muscle bound thug.

In the black community there was already a very fertile ground for sowing the seeds of discontent between the common man and the monied man. Poor blacks were never too trustful of blacks who had money. Generally this was due to the same kinds of self-gratifying class distinctions that stratify any group. Still, the "dichty" Negro was a perfect target in the years after Malcolm X and the big bad black militants who weren't showing themselves as "credits" to the race.

In 1972, Cicely Tyson, star of *Sounder*, attacked the blaxploitation fare saying, "There is nothing realistic about any of these films. They're fantasy; super-this and super-that. Totally unreal. The psychological effects that I'm concerned about are the ones on the kids. They're being affected by these negative images.''

Black psychiatrist Alvin F. Poussaint saw balxploitation films as "cheap thrills that degrade blacks! These movies glorify criminal life," Poussaint claims, "and encourage in black youth misguided feelings of machismo that are destructive to the community as a whole.''

But the big guns from the big studios struck back. Richard Lederer, vice president of advertising and publicity for Warner Brothers Studios defended the film *Super Fly*, or at least his studios' participation in the film by saying, " . . . we didn't make that movie, *blacks* did. Two Harlem dentists financed it and offered it to us. The images? Blacks who know tell us that in the ghetto, the pusher is a hero to the kids. Street blacks and nonbleeding-heart blacks say this is the only reasonable goal that black youth can aspire to.''

It was the kind of rhetoric that shifted blame, justified and celebrated incompetence by taking as expert any statements by anyone with dark skin who happens to be illiterate and so-called bad. But the films had redefined bad. "Bad" didn't mean the same as it did in the streets. For white and a great many supposedly black filmmakers a bad black man was one who broke the white man's laws and wouldn't take no shit from no one. They never gave these great heroic mannequins in black leather the "knowledge" which would lead them from battle in the streets with symptoms—crime, drugs, etc., to the source of the oppression that helped the symptoms to gain strength—racism.

Dick Gregory captured the essence of the quirk which

drives white people to believe that they somehow can peep anything they turn an eye to. "You gotta say this for the white race—its self-confidence knows no bounds. Who else could go to a small island in the South Pacific where there's no poverty, no crime, no unemployment, no war, and no worry and call it a "primitive society?"

The black films had all but taken the bite out of black theater which was developing in small storefronts and aging film houses that had lost all commercial value to the absentee landlords. Film was what was happening. Niggers got over on the white man and the audience didn't have to think. All they had to do was kick back and be jived.

The blaxploitation film gave a false statement of what life was really about in the teaming ghettoes of America and false solutions to the misread problems.

But it wasn't a new happening. It was a rerun of the game that Hollywood and the Broadway stage had run on blacks before, in the twenties and the thirties and the forties, and even before that.

Even when aggression was left in, it was misdirected. And while those blacks who were working saw themselves as simply paying a few dues until they could get to that place where they could do their own thing, there were others, like Paul Robeson, who knew the truth— you can't keep picking the cotton and hope to own the plantation.

Robeson, like Pryor, snubbed Hollywood. Neither of them was about to participate in their own degradation. "In the early days of my career as an actor," said Robeson, explaining his break from films, "I shared what was the then prevailing attitude of colored performers— that the content or form of a play or film scenario was of little or no importance to us. What mattered was the opportunity, which came so seldom to our folks, of having a part—any part—to play on the stage or in the movies.''

Robeson understood the ''Black First'' syndrome that held black America in a death grip. It didn't matter, just so long as a black man was getting over. Only the sharpest of the group could see that these so-called door-opening firsts were really nothing more than stop gaps. The poor, racist black film never opened the door for more creative efforts. They were making money. How can you improve on success?

''Later I came to understand that the colored artist,'' Robeson admitted, ''could not view the matter simply in terms of his individual interests, and that he had a responsibility to his people who rightfully resented the traditional stereotyped portrayals of colored people on stage and screen. So I made a decision. If the Hollywood and Broadway producers did not choose to offer me worldly roles to play, then I would choose not to accept any other kind of offer.''

No other kind of offer was forthcoming. It was to be expected. Americans, whites anyway, were not prepared to see the black race as it was. Such an opportunity would have too drastic an impact on the false light in which white Americans wanted, and want, to continue to see themselves.

The roles did not come because there was still much confusion, even among the ranks of black Americans, as to what kinds of roles truly reflected what was happening in black American life and culture. There were blacks denying other blacks the right to life in literature and film. There were those blacks who did not believe that there was anything even resembling culture in the black experience, including the blues, spirituals, poetry, gospel music and jazz.

And these folk were to be found at every economic and class level in the black race. All those so-called black cultural artifacts were simply horrible reminders of the degradations of slavery and poverty. They should be forgotten.

Novelist James Baldwin explained that "the American idea of racial progress is measured by how fast I become white. It is a trick bag, because they know perfectly well that I can never become white."

Though the blaxploitation films pointed damning fingers at those blacks who were trying to be white, the films never gave an accurate enough picture of what it was to be black, and therefore made no point at all.

But blacks were demanding their share of the pie. They were asking for their rightful share of access to the industry. Just how many coons, mammies, drunks, shuffling bumpkins, dichty Negroes trying to be white, prostitutes and sassy children that statistically worked no one ever said. It really didn't matter. It didn't happen then or later. The game played on.

The one place where a black cultural thing was happening was in the theater groups who could not find large audiences. There, at least, the actor and writer were beyond the control and dictations of a black middle class trying to forget the black part of their experience, or a white "cultured" class trying to reach out to touch other cultures—when they really liked to compare events with their own, using their own yardstick.

Pryor's art was evolving to that stage where it was becoming theater. It had never been enough for Pryor to simply tell jokes. Punch lines were not Pryor's bag.

He saw situations and these, often, could not be described. They had to be acted out. Pryor saw that the combination of dialogue and physical movement would best deliver the message that he was out to deliver. A message that he could not introduce to the main stages in America.

Mark Jacobson writes, Pryor's "using the word 'nigger' was the masterstroke. It aced him out of the mainstream, plus it made it quite clear where his racial allegiance lay. Everyone knows white people are not allowed to say that word."

Most of the flap was directed at Pryor's use of The Word, missing entirely what Pryor was really all about. McPherson wrote, Pryor "returned to the people and the comic situations he knew intimately.

He still did commentary, but his approach was altogether different. Instead of remaining aloof from his characters, Pryor became them, moving beyond interpretation to total integration of himself and his materials."

"Wherever I am," Pryor said, "they be laughing at the same shit, so I know we all know what's happening. I say, 'Well, now, Huey (Newton) done went crazy. Whipped his tailor 'cause the pants was too long.' And they laughed all over 'cause they knew who I was talking about. They knew about all the niggers who died following after him, and here he is beating up a tailor."

Pryor rapped about the things that he knew and the things that his audience saw and did on a daily basis. He knew them and it made his work real.

"They are alternately described as obscene," wrote Martin Weston, *Ebony* magazine writer, "but surely Pryor's reenactments of conversations are rarely more ribald than standard ghetto street vernacular. He simply doesn't censor the stories he retells, and he gives detailed, if expanded versions. He uses a method that is a subtle blend of the language and physical style of common people put into spontaneous skits that can at once be hilarious and horrendous. Pryor doesn't tell jokes; he relates incidents.''

It made sense. There were no thriving stages in the black community. But Pryor's brand of theater was perfectly suited to the places where black folk went to escape and be entertained. In the nightclubs and the bars Pryor was unrestricted by social convention, tradition, apathy. Pryor did his thing the way he wanted to.

"By the time I get to the mike," Pryor said, "the energy is so high I wouldn't care if a dude in the audience has a heart attack. All they could do is carry him out because I'm going to finish."

That kind of affirmation takes some of the steam out of the hot wind blowing about Pryor's unpredictability. Maybe what some folks want him to do, or expect him to do, are things that Pryor is just not up for doing.

While Pryor was really into what he was doing in the clubs throughout the country, making as much as $300,000 a year on the circuit which included many college campuses, he found that his act, as it was, just wasn't enough. The discovery came on the heels of his standout performance as Piano Man in Motown's extravaganza, *Lady Sings the Blues*.

The role was perfect for the Pryor magic that has created a sort of everyman who, while victim of his own and society's misdeeds, somehow can generate, from within himself, the energy to confront and even best the chaos that surrounds and imprisons him. Pryor had found a new arena, a spotlight for his people that he quickly developed a respect for.

100

The Motown epic attempted to cover the life of Billie Holiday. It was nothing more or less than a romanticized version of a very tragic experience. But it opened the door to Pryor. While others may point to the stars, Diana Ross and Billy Dee Williams, Pryor fans would scream out that the humorist stole scene after scene, becoming the only vibrant actor in the otherwise misleading film on the blues songstress.

"That showed me a lot about films," says Pryor of his role in *Lady Sings the Blues*. "I'd been working in clubs before groups of 300 people doing my thing and was happy with it until that movie. It put me into another perspective."

Piano Man was a step upward from the small parts he had in the 1967 spoof *Busy Body*, and the 1968 American International production, *Wild in the Streets*, where Pryor played a teenage musician. *Variety* pointed out that Pryor registered "strongly" as Piano Man who is beaten to death by dope dealers.

Pryor also proved to his detractors that he could be depended on to perform when the right role presented itself. Pryor moved to Hollywood to pursue a career in films. He had given up on television. At least he thought he had.

In 1972 Stax Records gave a benefit performance at the Los Angeles Memorial Coliseum. Linked with the then-annual Watts Festival, the performance was filmed by Columbia and released in film form as *Wattstax*. Pryor monologues linked together the acts that made up the bill.

Time reviewer Jay Cocks wrote that Pryor's material in *Wattstax* "wrings laughs from . . . shared frustration and humiliation. His stories of everyday hassling, of being regularly rousted by the cops, are spun out in street jargon with a kind of furious cool. What makes the jokes sting is not punch lines but lethal accuracy.''

Pryor was really getting into his niggerness. He raised the banner on high and did his people at every opportunity. And people looked and tried to listen, though a lot still did not understand.

Pryor copped the role of a pimp in the 1973 Cinerama production of *The Mack*. Critic Judith Crist gave Pryor "a better than average" for his performance in the blaxploitation film.

Pryor's presence saved many of the films from total banality but did little to give any real worth to them. More importantly they gave Pryor the opportunity to develop his film presence, to further explore his people in a completely different context.

In 1973, *Time* reviewer Jay Cocks wrote of Pryor's appearance in *The Hit*, which starred Billie Dee Williams. "Pryor's humor pierces through his characterization to mock the whole movie with energy and finesse.''

Uptown Saturday Night was Pryor's next venture. Directed by Sidney Poitier, the first of a series, the film was released in 1974 by Warner Brothers. Produced at a cost of $2.1 million, it grossed more than $9 million at the box office.

Bill Cosby, who starred in the production said, *Uptown Saturday Night* "is the first first-class comedy that black people will be able to see. It's clean; the material is clean, no foul language whatsoever. You can take anybody from your seven-year-old to your 87-year-old to see it, and they're gonna have a ball.''

Pryor played the role of Sharp Eye Washington, a less than angelic private detective, in *Uptown*. Reviewer Penelope Gilliatt said in the *New Yorker*, "The quick action and the non-stop dialogue are like a blackface parody of a white fast-talking thirties comedy, mixed with uniquely black bad-taste jokes about blacks which take one back to the old days of the Apollo Theatre.''

It seemed that the saving grace for these films was that they were ''bad-taste'' jokes by and about blacks, something very new in the industry. But, it was not Pryor. Not the Richard Pryor who was into his people. Pryor was reaching out and testing the water in all directions. The rumor was out that Pryor really wasn't so crazy after all. He was a hot property.

Pryor returned to television, a medium he had vowed to avoid as it ''degraded'' him. He did a *Tonight* show with Bill Cosby and out-improved his one-time idol. He was on the comeback trail, learning all there was to know about television, and finally getting a major break by working with Lily Tomlin.

''I got some practice writing the Lily Tomlin show,'' Pryor said, later. ''We had outside limits with all that shit. A lot of things we wanted to put in we couldn't. Yah. The earth of it was cut away. As it was growing, someone had these shears . . . snap, cuuuut, cut, cut. It was like silly shit that they cut, shit that probably wouldn't mean nothing bad. It was a waste.''

The censors objected to a skit where Pryor and Lily, as small children, discuss their bodies. ''I felt ridiculous,'' Pryor recalled to David Felton. ''My kid couldn't get into it. He said, 'I have titties bigger than your titties . . . boys have titties—first, boys have titties . . . then girls . . . ' And they said, 'No, we can't have that.' So I can't go onstage and it be in my mind that this kid can't say something, 'cause this kid is wrecked, as a kid.''

Pryor's characters had to be real, as they were in life.

He could do them no other way. He became them and they spoke through him. They would not restrict their language, it wouldn't be honest.

More than once Pryor has thrown up his hands and raised his voice saying, "I can't do no more." More than once that affirmation was misunderstood as being due to his "craziness" while Pryor knew that they were messing with his art.

Felton wrote "television has given these religious fanatics complete control over the language. There isn't a celebrity on television, from Dan Rather to Wolfman Jack, who's not forced to talk like these nuts—these queers!—who's not forced daily to perform unnatural acts, simply to be allowed to "communicate."

Pryor was turned-off by the restrictions but found that "watching Lily work was like watching someone give birth to shit. It really knocked me out. It was a turn-on."

Tomlin's praise of Pryor was equally high. "To me," Tomlin said, "Richard is separate from anybody else. See, when I think of Richard, like the hours I've spent with him, and I see him improvise and tell me about his life, or people he's known, or whatever impressions he's had, or little moments and fragments and things, you know, it's like . . . so *uplifting*."

Pryor had some of the same visions that Tomlin was blessed with. There was a similarity, though Pryor was more into improv.

Pryor "perceives (life) humanistically," Tomlin said. "It's like believing that we're all worth something, you know, when everything around us tells us that we're not really."

Felton wrote "they have introduced a version of comedy that goes beyond laughter, certainly way beyond the escapist entertainment we are used to seeing in nightclubs and on television.

"It's real theater," Felton explained, "a theater of the routine, the blemished, the pretentious, the lame—the common affairs and crutches of common people. Watching Lily and Richard perform is like watching yourself and all victims of human nature onstage; it can be painful and it can be exhilarating."

Common man? Maybe that distinction would fit Tomlin's people, who she described as being "all like humans," saying further, "Everybody had these incredble highs and terrible lows, everybody was afraid of something. They could be real petty and ugly, or they could be just real beautiful and uplifting and have wonderful little quirky moments where they made you laugh and other moments where you just hated them. And I saw that nobody knew anything. Nobody knew any answer to anything."

Pryor's folk were less quaint, less uplifting. Pryor was not simply painting a slice-of-life. He was seeing life in a very special way, which made him the artist, and reproducing it "accurately" but in such a way as to make a statement.

It is one thing to simply have a drunk or junkie say, "I am what I am because I couldn't cope with what the white man put on me." There's truth there, maybe one-sided, but it spotlights the junkie and the drunk as simple weaklings. It is quite another thing for Pryor's drunk to say, "Boy, you know what your problem is? You don't know how to deal with the white man. I do, that's why I'm in the position I am in today."

Pryor's people don't have little "quirks." Pryor's people are at war. They are oppressed. And while he never lets them ignore their own complicity in that oppression, he is very concerned with driving home the fact that many of these so-called common people know what the hell is really going on. And if they know what the hell is going on that moves them a step or two above the herd classification applied to them from outside.

Pryor says, "You look at them—some brothers and sisters who can't read, some who may have their combs sticking in their heads, or a big fat black woman with hair going every which-way—but when you live with them and hear them talk, you know that they are some of the smartest people on the planet because they know stuff that people out at those institutes at Yale and Harvard are trying to get."

Of his closeness to his people, Pryor said, "I don't think you do impressions of somebody you hate. If it is hate, it's some kind of admiration for something; the worst in the best, and the best in the worst."

No, Pryor's folk are not common. And they are no dark-skinned versions of Lily's people. Pryor's people have a special knowledge which developed out of a tragically, brutally abnormal set of circumstances. That special knowledge separates them from the herd and gives them a special insight—peeping power—into many things. Because of this Pryor's people often have a greater depth and purpose than those characters created by other comedians who have been compared to him. Pryor's people are not just funny. Because of that Pryor ran into major obstacles with the television industry who really wanted to use Pryor's talents.

"I do like to work on television," Pryor said, "but they say, 'No, we have to have laughter in there.' I say 'Don't you think people are sophisticated enough to enjoy something without being told when to laugh?' The laughter is in yourself. If you don't want to laugh you don't have to laugh; you could just be enjoying something. You don't have to laugh because somebody in the audience is laughing.''

Pryor was asking too much of a television audience weened on laugh tracks which spotlighted the punch lines so that audiences would know when it was time to ''enjoy'' themselves. While he wanted to separate himself from the herd, most folk found it safe to wait until they were told something was funny. And the great majority of them didn't even speak the language he was using. Maybe Pryor was pushing his style too hard. Maybe he should tone down, cool off, ''crossover''—it was the new game in town. The business minds found that an artist, black that is, could make a great deal more money if he could get white folks to buy his product. Pryor didn't care about the money. He was working on his thing.

''I want to drop things,'' Pryor explained to David Felton, ''try to develop new shit. All the things I talk about is experience, of somebody's or mine, or some story somebody told, or something in the papers and the news. What people really be thinking and don't say, you know—that's what I usually try to do; and then they laugh, 'cause they say, 'Yeah, I think that.' ''

Pryor knew exactly where his money was coming from. He knew what they wanted. He knew what they didn't want to see and hear. He knew what they were thinking and he knew what he wanted them to be thinking.

''I don't want people to be able to take me for granted,'' Pryor said. He doesn't want his audience to ''feel safe.'' Why? '' 'Cause they're gonna have to deal with me,'' Pryor said, '' 'cause I'm gonna say some shit maybe make them think, too. 'Ah he tricked us. I

107

thought he wouldn't hurt us.' ''

Sometimes Pryor was cold, vicious, like in his routine dealing with the kidnapped heiress, Patricia Hearst: "I'm sorry about her, though, 'cause a dumb white bitch with a bunch of niggers just drives you nuts. I know them niggers is ready to get rid of that ho'. She'll do anything—I'll bet she's doin' some helluva tricks, trying to pysch 'em out and shit. I'll bet the bitch is really dumb enough to do that.''

Sometimes Pryor's bits are met with stoney silence, as the audience shifts, toys with drinks, wondering if maybe they had missed something—the funny part. But they know quickly enough that they haven't.

Suffering was part of the game. Pryor said, "You've got to hurt to be funny.'' According to Pryor, he had suffered a great deal. Still a lot of fiction and fantasy seemed to be mixed with the facts of Pryor's life.

In 1973 he wrote an autobiographical screenplay, *This Can't Be Happening To Me*. In the screenplay the character Richard approaches his Mother, a prostitute, while she is screwing a white trick. Richard is supposedly dying, and is hallucinating.

"Why is this happening to me?'' Richard asks of his mother.

"Life is like that, Richard,'' she answers. "That's the way life goes. Sometimes things just go down that way.''

"Is it really good?'' the Trick asks while screwing her

"Oh honey,'' she lies, "there ain't a white man in the world can fuck as good as you.''

Richard's father is watching the scene through the keyhole.

Heavy fare for television. It was where Pryor was headed. Or maybe it was where his drugs were taking him? Maybe he was suffering from a serious case o drugs-and-booze-induced paranoia. Many would like to think so. It would explain away some of the guilt that goes with a Pryor performance.

But times were not altogether happy for Pryor though he copped two Emmys for the work he did on the Lily Tomlin specials. He had proven his talent while adding to his already legendary reputation for driving other people up the wall. It was an attitude which would haunt him in the coming years as he tried to expand his work in the film industry.

A part of the answer to Pryor's seemingly growing madness might be found in a routine he perfected in 1974, which finds him speaking to an inner voice which charges: "You ain't no nigger, you ain't no nigger, you ain't no nigger. You . . . are . . . a being. A beautiful . . . be-*ing*. Can you dig be-eee-eee-ing? As opposed to . . . not being?" And the voice continues, "You been lyin' back, posin' an' shit, bullshittin' motherfucker, tell you're *Dead* tonight. You are gonna *die* - me or you, *one* of us is gonna survive."

"I can't talk," Pryor stammers under pressure from the mysterious voice.

"Motherfucking right you can't talk," the voice counters. " 'Cause you're full of shit nigger. Can you dig it?"

And Richard cries out, "Ooooo-woooo-wooo-wha-a-in-the-fuckishappening-to-meeeeeeee?"

And the voice answers, "You becoming a man. You just born. But I'm afraid . . . you won't be a nigger no more. But you won't be ignorant, either . . . The truth everlasting."

It echoed his performance the last night on the stage the Aladdin Hotel when he asked, "What the fuck am I doing here?" Maybe he found out. But was the rest the world ready for it?

Looks like what drives me crazy
Don't have no effect on you.
But I'm gonna keep on at it
'til it drives you crazy, too
L. Hughes

Chapter 6: Crazy Nigger!

"I was in jail too, man . . . It's cold-blooded in jail. Nixon wouldn't have lasted two days. They'd turn him out . . . They give niggers time like it's lunch down there. You go down there lookin' for justice; that's what you find: just us!"

1974 wasn't exactly one of Pryor's better years. Still, from the ashes of chaos he managed to salvage enough precious stones to land him a few successful movie roles, and a platinum album which won him a Grammy and a few other awards.

The album was *That Nigger's Crazy*. It was an accusation that bubbled from the crowd at Don Cornelius' *Soul Train* in San Francisco. While audience's saw him as crazy, Pryor was probably more in control of himself and what he was about than he had been at any other time in his career.

The label was a catchy one. And it did seem to fit Pryor who, while some blacks had accepted that the great revolution was a thing of the past, was still throwing stones at the enemy. Pryor knew that many things may have changed but a great deal was still the same.

Most of Pryor's troubles stemmed from mistakes he made during his "period of irresponsibility" in the early years of his career. Somehow the cool-runner from Peoria, Illinois, had forgotten to give Uncle Sam his share of the booty that he collected from 1967-1970 before he kissed Vegas goodbye.

On March 14, 1974 Richard Pryor was indicted by a Federal Grand Jury for failure to file income taxes on income he earned from 1967-1970 which amounted to $250,000.

"That was no little trouble," Pryor told an interviewer. "I owed them money . . . Those motherfuckers wanted some of my ass."

They got some of Pryor's money—$2500. But all in all he got off light. The initial fine was $10,000; light financially that is. IRS also wanted a piece of Richard Pryor's ass which they got commencing June 4, 1974 and lasted a period of ten days in Los Angeles County jail.

"They kept me in 'protective custody,' " Pryor said, "so I couldn't mingle with the other prisoners. Said they were afraid I would try and escape, or the other prisoners would take me for a ransom so they could escape, shit like that.

"After that experience," Pryor said, "you don't have to wonder about how the Nazis did it—it's happening here. It was degrading, horrible. When I got out I ran immediately home and did the *That Nigger's Crazy* al-

114

bum. Got my first gold record."

It was an important album. Pryor was ready. His mind was in perfect sync with the situations he introduced on *That Nigger's Crazy*.

He was raw, "I'm gonna fuck you tonight, baby," says a Pryor drunk who has just been beaten in a barroom fight, "you can believe that shit." He passes out on his wife, a terrible ego blow to those who could relate.

He was real. "Boy, don't ever kiss no pussy," an Uncle warns. "I couldn't wait to kiss a pussy," Pryor confides. "He'd been wrong about everything else."

He explains the language differences. "I see older people in the audience going, "umph, umph, umph, you oughta be ashamed of yo'se'f junior."

"Winos ain't afraid of nuthin' but runnin' out of wine," said Pryor, and then he introduces one to Dracula. "Say, nigger, you with the cape. What you doin' peekin' in them people's window? What your name, boy? Dracula? What kind of name is that for a nigger? Where you from, fool? Transylvania? I know where it is, nigger. You ain't the smartest motherfucker in the world, even though you the ugliest . . . Why don't you get your teeth fixed, nigger—that shit hanging all out your mouth. This is 1975, boy. Git yo' shit together. What's wrong with yo' nat'ral? You got to be home 'fo the sun come up? You ain't lyin' motherfucker. See yo' ass in the day yo' liable to get arrested. You want to suck what? Some blood? Wha- you some kind of freak, boy? An ugly freak?! You ain't suckin' nuthin' here, junior."

On the police, a group Pryor is not fond of: "Cops put a hurtin' on yo' ass. They really degrade you. White folks don't believe that shit . . . that the police be degrading you. *White folks talk* 'Aw C'mon those beat-ings—those people were resisting arrest—I'm tired of this harassment of police officers.' The police live in your neighborhood. Nigger got to be talkin' 'bout (loudly) 'I am reaching into my pocket for my license 'cause I don't want to be no motherfuckin' accident.''

Pryor copped the label "crazy" because he was telling it like it was. He was not backing down, as one of his characters who was forced to "unball his fist" or "take the bass out of his voice." Pryor was speaking in many voices. Some of them hard, mean. He was not pulling punches. He was standing ground, and for that he was called crazy. A sad state of affairs for a man who was telling the truth.

. But Pryor accepted the title. It fit, he thought. At least it meant big dollars which would help him main-tain the kind of independent action that was responsible for his being crowned crazy.

Novelist Toni Morrison wrote, "Humor provides a frame and a distance and a kind of stability. High tragedy is not possible; the only other recourse is irony or that sardonic quality that makes it possible to see things clearly."

Pryor was right there with sharp irony. His humor was indeed sardonic. He chilled people with the truth. And many, if not all, laughed. They had to. It helped to buffer them from the cold hard truth.

Pryor had captured black folks, and the absurdity of their world, with such accuracy that he was awarded an honorary Ph.D. in Black Street History by the students of San Jose State College in California.

Joel Dreyfus, in a review for the Washington *Post*, said that Pryor's *That Nigger's Crazy* "moved the development of his comedy to the creation of particular characters" who "transcend the stereotypical situations in which they are located and become the archetypes with which all black people are familiar."

More than that Pryor was putting something on everybody's mind. That is the nature of his art which was more and more outgrowing the small clubs where he plied his trade.

Pryor had learned to love working in film. It was a more comfortable medium than television, with less restrictions—though the roles were not always so attractive. Pryor entered what turned out to be a very profitable, while not altogether agreeable, association with comic Mel Brooks, and the western spoof *Blazing Saddles* was born.

Pryor earned an American Writers Guild Award and the American Academy of Humor Award for his contribution to *Blazing Saddles*. But it is still a sore point with him. One he does not like to discuss.

"They used me," Pryor said of his association with *Blazing Saddles* and Mel Brooks. "And it's a thorn in my heart about it."

The furor came out of Pryor's not being chosen for the lead role in the film—Cleavon Little starred as the black sheriff—when he felt that the role was promised to him.

Rumors abounded but a major one suggested that Pryor was not given the role because of his so-called "coke rep" which would not sit well with the American movie audiences. Middle America was again riding Pryor's ass.

Brooks denied that Pryor was rejected from the role because of his supposed overindulgence in coke and booze, or for any other reason, suggesting that the studio was probably afraid to go with an unknown.

Pryor's contributions to *Lady Sings the Blues* were still unknown as the film had not as yet been released while *Blazing Saddles* was in production.

Brooks explained to *Rolling Stone* in 1974 that Pryor was not really ever considered for the starring role though it may have seemed that way "when we were writing it, before I even, you know, thought of anybody. When we were writing it, it was so natural; I mean he was just acting out so many things so beautifully. But it was just simply out of the question. They weren't gonna risk all that money on an unknown."

Pryor tells quite a different tale when he's talking about it. He claims that Brooks wanted him to have the starring role but bowed to pressure. He also points out that the script really was worked out from his own screenplay *Black Bart*.

"That movie wasn't funny when I first got there," said Pryor. "I told Mel Brooks to put in the farting and shit. *Blazing Saddles* wouldn't have never been blazing except they farted in a lot of saddles."

Brooks suggested that Pryor would really be great when he managed to "settle down" and shake off a few "ah, emotional traits."

"Brooks seemed at times to be praising with faint damns," wrote Felton who interviewed Brooks.

Those "emotional traits" read "crazy" by many were not something that Pryor was about to shake. In fact, it was because of Pryor's emotional traits that he was so successful.

"Maybe I'm afraid of easing me into a corner I can't get out of," said Pryor in 1974. "Maybe I'm gonna find someday that I've given up so much of me that the real me is hiding somewhere and no one can find me, not even me. Maybe I'm afraid of never finding that inner security, that inner, spiritual peace."

Observers would be the first to charge that Pryor had not given up enough of himself, that raw, angry, obscene self that won't make people laugh. In 1974 he was fined $500 in Richmond, Virginia, after being arrested on charges of disorderly conduct and use of obscenity during an appearance. It was like putting clothes on the statue of Venus.

In May of 1974 Pryor showed another side, one that few people attributed to him, by successfully working for the temporary release of eight inmates from the Lorton Correctional Complex, Lorton, Virginia. The inmates performed as the Inner Voices, and Pryor had caught their act while performing at the institution. He promised the group that they would appear on the Apollo stage with him, and he kept that promise. Somehow it isn't the way a dope fiend would operate.

In 1975 *That Nigger's Crazy*, reissued by Reprise Records for Warner Brothers, won the NATRA (National Association of Television and Radio Announcers) award for Comedian of the Year and music industry trade magazine *Record World's* award for comedy Album of the Year.

Pryor was going full steam. In August of 1975 he struck again with his Reprise/Warner release, *Is It Something I Said*? The album cover pictures Pryor bound to a pile of kindling and surrounded by hooded figures who are carrying torches. Pryor's expression is blameless.

The humor is raunchy but true. He cripples the male ego with, "I'm gonna go out and find me some new pussy!" And the wife counters, "If you had two more inches of dick you'd find some new pussy here." *Ouch*!

Or the new niggers, the Vietnamese who are boarded

at Army camps until they can learn how to become good citizens by learning to say, "Nigger!"

Produced by David Banks and scripted by Pryor, except for "Just Us" routine, he claims to have "stolen from Paul Mooney, *Is It Something I Said*? was recorded live at The Latin Casino in Cherry Hill, New Jersey.

It was on this album that Pryor admitted to his excessive use of cocaine. "I snorted cocaine for about fifteen years—with my dumb ass. I must of snorted up Peru." It wasn't a boast. It was an admission of weakness rather than bravado. It was what made Pryor so special.

The album covered Pryor's stint in jail for tax evasion: "I went to jail for income tax evasion. I didn't know a motherfuckin' thing about no taxes. I tol' the judge that. 'Yo' honor I forgot.' *Judge*: 'You'll remember next year, nigger!' "

"You got to be funny in jail," Pryor quips, "or give up the bootie . . . I made niggers laugh all day long . . . keep their minds off the bootie."

Pryor introduced Mudbone: " . . . an ol' man who dip snuff an' he sit in front the barbecue pit and he spit . . . That was his job. I'm pretty sho' that was his job, 'cause that's all he did. But he'd tell stories, fascinating stories."

And then Pryor lays on a bit of truth with a delicate stroke, "You learn something when you listen to old people. They ain't all fools. You don't get old being no fool." (And *Roots* hadn't even hit yet.)

The bad days seemed to be behind Pryor. His albums were a success. He was getting offers from a few television shows for guest spots but most of all his motion picture work was growing.

120

It was in 1976, success teasing him, that Pryor made one of the wisest decisions of his career. He met and signed as his manager a young Atlanta lawyer who had once been law partners with the mayor of Atlanta, Maynard Jackson. The young lawyer, David McCoy Franklin, took Pryor's career and financial dealings in hand and it became a positive and financially secure association.

Franklin attended American University Law School and learned to wheel and deal in the entertainment industry, though he took time out to become financial chairman and fund raiser for Jackson's mayoral campaign.

Franklin knew the business well and lifted a heavy burden from Pryor's slumped shoulders, giving the artist more time to devote to his craft. Even more, it was through Franklin's efforts that Pryor received contract guarantees that previously had been only given to white performers.

David Franklin quickly worked out a $3 million dollar deal with Thom Mount of Universal Studios which gave the studios "first right of refusal" for six motion pictures by Pryor. Pryor had the option to choose whether or not he would perform in the films while still being free to act in non-Universal projects.

"We believe," said Mount, "it is possible to make money on class A pictures that not only star black people, but are made by black people."

Pryor said, "Well, I guess that means if these movies don't make money a whole lot of niggers gonna be in trouble."

If nothing else, Pryor knew that little had changed in that regard. No matter what he might say or do as an artist, as Richard Pryor, he was still somehow representing the race, even though he was not out to be a leader, but to find Richard Pryor and inner security.

Franklin was a major asset to Pryor in more than a financial way. Franklin was the buffer that protected Pryor, not so much from himself—Pryor could take care of Pryor—but from those people outside who would do harm.

"I have no financial problems," said Pryor to Bob Lucas of *Jet* magazine. "I eat all the time now. I have more shoes than I have feet and I have another pair of pants. David Franklin is a genius of an attorney and deal maker. I know I couldn't have gotten this far with a white manager or agency concerned with their percentages first.

"We, David and Pryor, operate independently. I like David's energy and his creative ability. He's not a greedy man. He's much smarter than anyone he's dealing with and he's not afraid of white people. I knew he was serious when he asked (them) for more money."

While Pryor did want the security that money could give him, he was not intimidated by money and respected that quality in others. Pryor was generous too. In 1977 he rewarded Franklin for his good work by presenting him with a $52,000 Rolls Royce. That same year Pryor popped for a modest but rambling ranch style house in Peoria for his grandmother on Mother's Day. Yes, he liked what the money could do.

The blaxploitation movie was gradually dying away. And those blacks who did work did so as side kicks or nondescript characters. Most didn't work. Pryor did. He had his choice of properties, considering the state of the industry, which hadn't changed much since the time of Paul Robeson.

Still, Pryor fumbled and stumbled into a project with

Fred Williamson, who wrote and directed a western spoof, *Adios Amgios*. They shot the film in nine days. It played as if it was a home movie shot in much less time.

"Tell them I apologize," said Pryor after the release of *Adios Amigos*. "Tell them I needed some money. Tell them I promise not to do it again."

And he didn't. His next series of pictures, though sometimes mediocore themselves, gave Pryor an opportunity to do his thing in grand style and write his own ticket in more ways than one.

The Bingo Long Travelling All-Stars and Motor Kings was one of two films Pryor did for Universal in 1976 in association with Motown. The film starred Billie Dee Williams, James Earl Jones, and Richard Pryor.

The film exploded out of the depression-choked Midwest of the late 1930s. It was a nostalgic and often comic look at the trials and tribulations of a group of black ball players who revolt against Negro League management. They form their own team under the leadership of Bingo Long, ace pitcher, played by Billie Dee Williams.

Pryor takes the role of Charlie Snow, an ambitious third baseman intent on cracking the majors. Snow is a game player who knows the game but fumbles at it. Snow tries passing for a Cuban and then an American Indian in an attempt to overcome his color which is holding him back. Like Piano Man in *Lady Sings the Blues*, Charlie Snow is sensitive, intense and gets beaten up and almost killed. He is victim.

The film was based on a book by William Brashler and adapted for the screen by Hal Barwod and Matthew Robbins. It was directed by John Badham and filmed in Macon, Georgia, primarily. It was not just another blaxploitation film. It was a fair attempt at putting together something meaningful. Pryor exploited the opportunity and was excellent.

Pryor was finding historical parallels to his people. He was linking them together across the decades, "rooting" them in their very real history.

But Pryor was still the "comic relief element." Or at least he was supposed to be. There wasn't anything funny about the beating Charlie Snow took or the death of Piano Man. He was not the leading man. Always someone's sidekick. Someone's foil. And while he was working steadily, it was probably a difficult time for Pryor who seemed to be saving other people's pictures, blacks and whites.

The Universal production of *Car Wash* which introduced Rose Royce's song of the same title needed a jolt of hot wax and Pryor was called into play as Reverend Rich. As the sharp, quick-tongued young, slick and big-monied cult leader, Pryor was surrounded by the up and coming Pointer Sisters.

It is rumored that the film, which covers a day in the lives of the people who work in a car wash, a motley array of characters concocted by an offbeat imagination, had to be re-edited to include more and more of Richard Pryor as the dap Reverend Rich. It is alleged Reverend Rich, as played by Pryor, lived. The rest of the movie was a bust before the re-editing job. Reverend Rich, as played by Pryor, lived. The rest of the movie was fantasy.

It was the Bicentennial year. America had survived for two hundred years as a democratic country. A free country. At least that was the pablum being fed to 200 million Americans and the rest of the world.

Pryor had something quite different to say about America's 200th birthday. He carefully reached into his gift bag and fashioned a work of art which he delicately wrapped and labeled, *Bicentennial Nigger*. It won Pryor another Grammy. And well it should have. It was his most powerful work to that time. The album stunned and jarred and told the truth.

Pryor was still scene stealing. But this time he was stealing America's thunder. He was keeping things in the proper perspective because no one was running cute one minute spots about how bad slavery was, and how deep the shit still was. It was a 'tata pie in the face of Lady Liberty. Dozen playing at its political best.

Even more, *Bicentennial Nigger* was a reaffirmation of Pryor's commitment to raising questions that plagued the American mind.

The loud voices had been silenced—Malcolm was dead, King was dead—but Pryor wasn't dead, nor were his people, who were ready to celebrate the big birthday bash.

In a most solemn and high sounding voice, Pryor's preacher announces, "We're celebrating 200 years of white-folks-kickin'-ass . . . White folks have had the essence of disunderstanding on their side . . . howsomever we offer this prayer . . . How long . . . will the bullshit . . . go on? How long will the bullshit go on? That is the eternal question."

"You all know how black humor started," says Pryor before unleashing the Bicentennial Nigger, "it started on slave ships. A cat was on the way over here . . . rowing. Dude say 'What you laughing about?' he say, 'Yesterday I was a king.' "

A drum rolls and the Bicentennial Nigger, 200-years-old, in blackface, stars and stripes painted on his forehead, his lips just as shiny, a white folks expression on his face . . . but he's happy " 'cause he's been here 200 years." His voice humble, he chuckles and snorts stupidly, yet he speaks, "I'm just thrilled to be here. I used to live to be a hundred and fifty. Now I die of high blood pressure by the time I'm fifty-two . . . that thrills me to death (he chuckles). They brought me over here on a boat.

There was 400 of us come over. (Chuckles and snorts.) 360 of us died on the way over here . . . (chuckles). I just love that . . . (chuckles) . . . it just thrills me to death . . . You white folks are just soooo good to us . . . (chuckles) . . . We got over here and another twenty of us died from disease . . . split us all up. Took my momma over that way, my wife over the other way . . . I don't know what I'm gonna do if I don't get 200 more years of this . . . (no chuckles) . . . Y'all white folks probably done forgat about it . . . (pause and the voice is no longer humble, or old, but threatening)—but I ain't gonna never forget."

The album complete, Pryor threw himself into his writing and film work. It was something he had developed a craving for and there was not enough work to satisfy his hunger.

Pryor had settled into his eight acre estate in Northridge, California, surrounded by 52 fruit trees and cut off from the frills and follies of the Hollywood crowd by a mountain range. He was comfortable, secure for the first time in his life. He was no longer paying rent. He owned the place.

Pryor was rich and comfortable and working. And his love life wasn't going so badly. He'd had liaisons with three women by 1976, and had fathered four children.

Bob Lucas wrote, "With each role, Pryor's fee goes up, putting him well on the way toward a goal he projected one and a half years ago when he confided that he

126

wants to be rich, saying, 'Everyone wants to be rich. Anyone who says he doesn't want to be rich is crazier than people say I am.''

Pryor spread some of the bread around. The $8,000 he received for taping his *Bicentennial Nigger* album at the Roxy in Hollywood was divided and donated in equal shares to the minor children of Jackie Wilson, a stricken singer, and to help defray some of the expenses incurred by comedian/turned activist Dick Gregory on his cross-country fund raising run.

Pryor also bought and donated 1000 tickets to the Los Angeles Branch of the NAACP so that they might enjoy an evening with celebrity writer Alex Haley.

"I'm fortunate," Pryor told Bob Lucas, "and mad, I hope I can do some good with it, really help somebody."

Pryor was in control, at least of his work. Maybe that inner voice was still dozen-playing with him, talking shit that he didn't want to hear but couldn't ignore. At least he had a better idea of where he had come from and what he was trying to do.

"Everyone said I dropped out," he told Lucas. "I didn't drop out. I just stopped so I could look things over and decide what to do.

"I was not happy with what I was doing," Pryor said, "and I said, well, this is time to quit; this was my decision about what kind of life I was going to have and I wasn't going to have the kind of life that they were going to give me. People can't give you a life. I wanted to carve mine out."

The blade is often jagged, tearing rather than cutting cleanly, but Pryor is indeed carving out his own life from the granite face of America.

"I think it's been a struggle for me," said Pryor, "because I had a chance to be white and refused. They offered me that every day." Of course he refused. To become white would have been to lose the very talent that was in so much demand, the ability to be deadly accurate and honest while being funny. It was a whole new thing that was solely Richard Pryor's creation, as he struggled to make it.

Felton said, "Richard Pryor has established himself as a rare and serious innovator, a perfectionist in the arts of comedy, mime, drama."

Pryor's next venture was a role in *Silver Streak*, a Gene Wilder film which Pryor stole. He was alive, vital, creating. He had seemingly cleaned up his life, if not his act.

Mark Jacobson was on the set of *Silver Streak* and wrote, everyone "seemed to be talking about how Richard hadn't missed a day of shooting, how he's never forgotten a line, how he hasn't been a problem of any kind."

Maybe it wasn't so much that Pryor hadn't become a "problem of any kind" but rather that no one had given him any problems.

"I'm through actively messing with my body," Pryor said, announcing that he was a vegetarian. He explained that his problems of the past were due to the fact that "I was a kid then. That was before I changed."

Pryor always said that he could do anything he wanted to do, cold turkey. Is that what he did? And if so, what was the catalyst? A woman maybe? But none had ever been able to tame him before. Or maybe it was a combination of things, his new home, his success, his rising fame.

David Franklin was right there working hard for Pryor and clearing away the obstacles which may have accounted for his fondness for drugs and booze. It was Franklin's job and he did it well.

"Ninety percent of the black artists are getting ripped off, explained Franklin. "The best service I could give them would be to take a machine gun and wipe out all the people around them and start over."

Franklin took an active role in straightening up Pryor's nose condition, "I told him," Franklin said, "that I wasn't interested in representing a junkie."

Whether Pryor straightened up for Franklin, family, friends or some inner voice is unimportant. Pryor did it and again managed to please the critics.

It is a spy movie on a train, the Silver Streak, which runs from Los Angeles to Chicago. It is burdened by murder, pretty girls and disguised crooks and brightened by Richard Pryor.

Claude R. Reed reviewed the film for *Unique* magazine, saying, "Right before the boredom puts you to sleep, enter: Richard Pryor . . . He flows so smoothly that it is apparent that he wrote some of his lines."

Pryor was doing more than just being a black face in the movies. He had done much toward changing the accepted stereotypes offering fleshed out people in their stead. But a great deal of his work was ignored or attacked by middle class black folk who did not know much about what they were putting down, more concerned about what some white folk might think of *them* than whether or not Pryor got his message across. The black censors could be just as narrow-minded and stupid as the whites.

"Movies are movies," defended Pryor, "and I don't think any of them are going to hurt the moral fiber of America and all that nonsense. The black groups that boycott certain films would do better to get the money together to make the films they want to see or stay in church and leave us to our work.''

Pryor arches his back quickly when his work is questioned, belittled, or restricted by noncreative people. It was the very thing that kept him away from television. Unfortunately for the shortsighted, their bantering would continue to take its toll.

But there were those who did see beyond the so-called ''mask of comedy'' and so through to that which Pryor was really about. Maureen Oth observed in *Newsweek* magazine, ''the black screen image as defined by Pryor has traveled 180 degrees from that of the shufflin' yes-ma'am Stepin Fetchit of 40 years ago.

''An argument can be raised in defense of Stepin Fetchit and Willie Best and Mantan Moreland and company, the black humorists and physical comics who paved the way not only for black actors and actresses but *white* comics who copied their material.''

Pryor was facing a new audience. They were young, upwardly mobile, career minded, and out for number one first. The Me-first generation was on the set, digging the films, sipping the drinks in the nightclubs and bistros. They had the bread. And they did not want to trip off of social problems. Cocaine, ah sure. But racism and such, no. There were those blacks who had grown tired of discussing the ''problem'' and the differences between blacks and whites. This crop of intellectuals were certain that such discussion only amplified the problems, changing nothing. Besides the kind of blacks Pryor was talking about were where they were through their own shortcomings. Why didn't they pull themselves out of the gutter, by themselves!?

The characters Pryor loved were often losers who fought back even though the odds were against them.

They were not muscular heroic figures who could beat, maim, protect. They resisted! Sometimes weakly, often after bending over further than the John Wayne types, but still they resisted, on their own terms. And while they could not fly and stop bullets and live, they were seldom pathetic people.

Pryor was moving toward that place where his people were revealing more and more about themselves. With each new discovery Pryor grew. It became harder and harder to tell where Pryor left off and his people began.

"Sometimes what appears to be real in my life isn't," Pryor said. "I'm still acting."

That encourages the question; how long has Pryor's shit been going on? Has he been conning the American public, black and white, with his bullshit? Is Pryor really some angelic drop-out from a seminary his rich and dichty parents shuffled him off to because he was trying to do the maid?

Pryor's off screen lifestyle, real or imagined, kept him in the public's eye. He was the only living rebel. Everyone else was copping out in their sordid attempts to cope. Pryor was doing whatever the hell *he* felt like doing, challenging the very gods of money themselves and *surviving*, something no one else had been able to do.

Pryor would not sell out, and the nigger wouldn't OD and die! He was like his people, vulnerable, yes, but still dangerous. "You got to bring ass to git ass!"

While no one could claim to have ever seen Pryor snort cocaine, or drink or pass out from either, the mystique was there. In America that's all that counts. Americans really believe that John Wayne was in the service.

Whether it was planned, real, or simply an overreaction on the part of a white controlled Hollywood at their failure to control the nigger, or seduce him with the traditional trinkets, is anyone's guess, but Pryor's way of life captivated an America which leered like *voyeurs* through Pryor's keyholes.

Gambling that Pryor would attract audiences, Warner Brothers entered into a six-film partnership with Pryor which would generate more than a million dollar-per-flick "piece of the action" for the funny man from Peoria.

A collection of Pryor's best was released for the album buying public as "*Greatest Hits.*" Pryor was busy elsewhere. He had films to do, *Greased Lightning, Which Way Is Up?, Blue Collar, The Wiz.* He was really living high on the cinematic hog.

But Pryor had not lost his perspective. He was concerned about what he was doing.

"If I do my work good," Pryor said, "I'll have the base to do something. It's up to me and my work to be excellent and if I can continue to make money at what I'm doing then the doors will open up to others the way Sidney Poitier and Bill Cosby have opened doors."

Too often those doors have slammed shut more quickly than they were opened. But no matter. Pryor was doing his best to open the doors the right way. He was going to snatch them off their very hinges so that they couldn't be shut again. He was still quite capable of stunning people even though they felt they had adjusted to his style.

A *Variety* critic caught a Pryor performance at the Los Angeles Shubert and wrote: "Pryor's language has become a meaningless ritual that hardly shocks anybody these days. He just uses those words as a rhythmic background to some exceedingly funny concepts. But he can still shock when he chooses.''

Audience's expected Pryor to use foul language and even anticipated it. It took some of the sting out of what Pryor was doing. The populace had become immune to some of his antics. It was one of the major reasons why Pryor developed such a great love for film. He had an opportunity to use tools that were not available to him on wax or in the small clubs, or on television. It was Richard Pryor in larger than life living color.

"Viewed from the perspective of American tradition," wrote James McPherson, "Richard Pryor is the first totally unselfconscious black comic to turn his perceptions—and language—on black people themselves. He forces them to look at their faults and laugh."

More importantly, McPherson says, "Assured of their humanity, he holds up before his audiences patterns of behavior which have evolved into somewhat rigid styles, and reminds them that they are only masks—and comic ones at that."

Greased Lightning, a Warner Brothers production, co-starred Richard Pryor and Pam Grier, with Max Julien, Cleavon Little and Bo Bridges filling out the cast. It was a *Richard Pryor* movie rather than a *black* movie which was somehow an advancement over even what Poitier had done because a great many people had been hard pressed to identify Poitier as black.

Atlanta Mayor Maynard Jackson and Georgia State Senator Julian Bond played minor parts in the film which was based on the life of Wendell Scott, champion race car driver who won the Grand Nationals in 1961.

Melvin Van Peebles, considered by some as the force who triggered the rush of Blaxploitation movies in the early '70s with his *Sweet Sweetback's Baadasssss Song*, was slated to direct the race car epic which was to be shot in Georgia.

Before filming was complete Van Peebles was fired because he allegedly was not making the film commercial enough. Van Peebles countered with "I would have made it more commercial if they had asked me."

Mike Schultz, a young black director who had scored well with *Cooley High* and *Car Wash*, took over the director's chair on the set of *Greased Lightning* which earned well over $10 million after it was released.

Wed in their roles on screen, Pryor and Grier developed into a hot item off screen. "Richard and Pam," reported Bob Lucas, "were acquainted before they went on location to shoot *Greased Lightning*. That friendship grew and blossomed into something deeper during weeks of work."

At a benefit in December of the previous year Pryor, who had bought a full page ad in the December issue of *Jet* magazine, celebrating *Kwanza*—Black Christmas ritual—announced that he was donating $5,000 to the organization of black actresses which went by the name Kwanza. Pryor also pledged $5,000 of Grier's money for her which suggested a more than casual link between the two stars. It was enough to whet the appetites of the Hollywood crowd.

Grier had already made a name in the early generation of black movies which starred her as the predecessor to *Wonder Woman*, taking the lead in a man's world.

In *Coffy, Foxy Brown* and *Sheba Baby*, Grier introduced a black woman the equal of *Shaft* and the better of most men.

"If you think about it," Grier explained, "you'll see she was the prototype for the more recent and very popular White Bionic and Wonder Women.

"I make no apologies for the women I created," Grier says. "Actually, I recreated. When I grew up I knew a certain kind of black woman who was the sole support of her family and who would, if you disrespected her, beat you into the cement."

Fortunately the role she had in *Greased Lightning* did not allow Grier to play "to the bone" the strong black woman who might have beat the less macho characters created by Pryor into the "cement." Pryor's characters struggled, ducked and dodged, sometimes ran in circles before they found the way. Grier's portrayals knocked down things, blasted holes in people, places and things, walked over or through obstacles.

"It's a very big thing," Pryor said of his relationship with Pam Grier. "I like her very much, and she likes me." They were seen together often, travelled as companions, and Pam hosted affairs at Pryor's Northridge mansion. It seemed that Pryor had found what he needed. That inner peace and financial security that he had set his sights on. And the work kept coming.

Which Way Is Up? was an especially important film in that it gave Pryor the opportunity to "flesh out" more than one of his people. It was a chance to play them one against the other, in context, in a real environment, or at least one that was blanched or colored by his audience's imagination. Pryor dressed the characters. There was no doubt how they were supposed to look. Film gave him that latitude.

Michael Schultz was again in the director's seat, with novelist Cecil Brown—*Lives and Loves of a Jiveass Nigger*—co-writing the screenplay with Carl Gottlieb.

The screenplay was loosely based on Lina Wertmuller's 1972 comedy *The Seduction of Mimi*. Initially a scenario about the life and loves of grape pickers, Pryor becomes an orange picker who, in very unheroic fashion, keeps a wife and mistress, while trying to survive and connive his way up the ranks of the union.

Pryor plays Leroy Brown, the conniving hero, opposite pretty Lonette McKee who plays his mistress, and Margaret Avery as his wife who happens to become pregnant by a less than honorable, collection plate conscious preacher, played by none other than Richard Pryor. Then there is the foul mouthed, dirty old man who applies wisdom to the sauce as Leroy Brown's father, played "to the bone," by Richard Pryor.

Encore Magazine selected Richad Pryor as best actor for the 1977 season because of his portrayals in *Which Way Is Up*? and *Greased Lightning*.

Newsweek said that Pryor had reached a sort of "crossroads" where he was "diffusing and defusing his fierce talent in muddled movies like *Silver Streak, Greased Lightning* and *Which Way Is Up*?

"One hopes," suggested *Newsweek*, "that, like his friend Lily Tomlin, Pryor can take control of what should be an extraordinary career."

"Take control." "Emotional traits." Subtle digs? Or were reviewers still not in touch with the product? On two of the films, *Greased Lightning* and *Which Way Is Up*?, there was black direction, Mike Schultz, and black writing, provided by Pryor on one and Cecil Brown on the other. What was the missing element? What did or didn't reviewers see?

Time reviewer John Skow, while impressed with Pryor as a talent, was critical, in an off-handed sort of way, of Pryor's characters. It is Skow's view which might shed some light on why some were still against Pryor's presentations, or at least refused to see all that

136

was happening.

"Pryor's characterizations," wrote Skow, "have nothing to do with the cool black humor of such modern comics as Bill Cosby and the late Godfrey Cambridge. He plays eye-rolling, foot-shuffling, minstrel-show darkies, with a bit of ghetto fast-mouth thrown in."

Skow recognized that the audience in attendance was having a good time, even though ninety percent black. Did he mean that he could not understand how they could laugh at such "Amos n' Andish" antics? Or did he mean that maybe he missed something, some nuance in the characterizations, or maybe some experience in his life which would have brought him into contact with them as human beings?

While the latter is probably true and lack of understanding is at the root of his observations, Skow probably believes that the images are really negative and nonexistent, carry-overs from the days of blackfaced minstrelsy.

Pryor was still working on two other films, *The Wiz* and *Blue Collar*. While *The Wiz*, a black version of Frank Baum's *Wizard of Oz*, might seem to verify Skow's opinion of Pryor's characterizations, *Blue Collar* was something quite different.

A Motown-Universal Production, *The Wiz* starred Motown's super star and ex-Supreme, Diana Ross. The adaption created a fantasy Land of Oz in the streets of New York where a Harlem school teacher had been swept away by a snowstorm. It carried a $20 million dollar budget to pay for the likes of Richard Pryor as The Wiz, Michael Jackson as the Scarecrow, Nipsey Russell as the Cowardly Lion, Mabel King as the Wicked Witch and Lena Horne as the Good Witch.

There was controversy from the very beginning. While some, especially a few blacks, were upset because they saw no need for a black version of anything white when there were enough black things around to do, there were those who were more concerned about Diana Ross's selection as the black Dorothy, a role made famous and classic by Judy Garland—a young Judy Garland. Some said Diana Ross was just too old. Others argued that the writer never described the original Dorothy. Age didn't matter.

It mattered enough so that a change of directors was in order. John Badham left as director saying he strongly "believed that it's a story of a little girl." He was not against Diana Ross, "but the rightness of a lady of her maturity playing a little girl."

Sidney Lumet who directed the hit *Network*, took over the directing chores of *The Wiz*.

"The film is not about a little girl at all," Ross said. "It's about a human being, and it's ageless and timeless and colorless, even though black people are doing it."

Color was still very much the issue, even in the middle-to-late '70s. It was a barrier that no black actor, writer, producer or director seemed to be able to best, though they continued to try.

"White people do films," said Ross, "and everybody identifies, and just because black people are doing this doesn't mean it's just about black people. Or even about little girls. What's going on underneath is about people."

Maybe so. Maybe it was about people. The audience's didn't get into it. And while some might say it flopped because it was black, there are those who would argue that it flopped because it wasn't black enough.

Pryor's characters always worked, even though they

138

often did not get through the thick blinders worn by whites, because they were real people. They came out of the lives of the people who make up Pryor's audiences. Fans are always rushing him identifying his characters as family members, friends, even themselves. There was no Land of Oz in Harlem and real niggers knew that.

Charles Champlin, reviewer for the *Los Angeles Times*, wrote, "The Wiz is at last Richard Pryor, camped out in a warehouse and reduced to a whining falsetto apology that is the most conspicuous waste of talent in *The Wiz*.

"I kept wishing he would say something rotten," wrote Champlin, "to pep up the proceedings."

Champlin described the film as "a considerable disappointment."

Playboy offered, "Even Richard Pryor, as The Wiz himself, and Lena Horne, as the good witch Glinda, are lost in the fruit salad of scenic effects for a fairy tale that has very little charm or innocence and virtually no Soul."

It was a multimillion dollar bomb that missed black folks and white folks. What happened?

Whatever happened, and social critics, especially those who are from the E. Franklin Frazier school of thought, would say that black Hollywood was too busy trying to please everybody, meaning white people especially and in particular, and in their fury, ended up pleasing no one at all.

Attitudes had changed in the land. Black folks did not want to be reminded of the nasty things in life. *Roots* quite successfully took some of the bitterness out of slavery by disguising villains, all in all replacing Pryor's kind of people with a nobler lot who survived slavery and all the hardships that followed without resorting to some of the sordid escapes and cons run by Pryor's kind of people.

It explained why white people were laughing at Pryor's people and not cringing from them as they once had done. They were nasty, crude, even self-destructive, but not dangerous.

In *Blue Collar* Pryor made certain that everyone understood where he was coming from. There was no mistaking the desperation, the urgency, the danger that rippled the muscles and tortured the souls of his people.

White folks had successfully insulated themselves from the *nigger of the sixties* who had scared the shit out of them with raised fists and bad talk. Blacks who did not want to be reminded of their obligations to themselves and to those who had shed blood and were continuing to shed blood in the streets had also built up a resilience to the Pryor insanity. Everybody knew that Super Nigger couldn't fly, and being a nigger wasn't *shit*.

If Pryor had softened his thrust and dulled his blade, he changed courses in *Blue Collar*. He groveled in the dark world of desperation, love, passion and came out smelling like a rose.

Pryor said: "I knew while we were doing it that we were doing something very good. The energy was right, and the actors are superb in terms of their art . . . There was a lot of pressure, and it was the hardest work I've ever done, but it came out well. Paul Schrader wrote the script and he directed it and did a good job."

Blue Collar was based on an idea by Sydney A. Glass which, *Playboy* writes, "brings forth a stinging, realistic drama about Detroit auto workers that is both persuasive and suspenseful."

Blue Collar starred Pryor, Harvey Keitel and the

powerful Yaphet Kotto. They are life's losers. They work gigs that come from nowhere and are going nowhere. They haven't even progressed to the level of "button pushers." They are the buttons that are pushed. They are part of the machinery, an expendable part. These aren't the same working stiffs that Pryor cavorted with in *Car Wash*. They were not funny. They were hapless, hopeless, dangling at the end of their rope, unable to cope with even the most trivial of life's problems.

The theme is summed up in this bit of dialogue: "They pit the lifers against the new boys, the blacks against the whites—they keep us in our place."

The words could have come from a prison script, that's how powerful the machine had become, how helpless the men who had become its slaves had grown. It was life. Not black life or white life, but life. Human life under some very crippling conditions. It was the stuff of which Richard Pryor was made - "the backside of life . . . where people saw things different than if you had money and were careful what you said."

The trio, auto workers, are driven to robbery. They storm the union office and only gain $600 for their efforts, and the additional burden of eluding gangster types whose top secret ledger has been swiped in the robbery. The movie ends in bloodshed and failure. The madness wins. And no one is laughing. That bothered Pryor. Not because he didn't want the film to end that way. "It changed my life," he said. "I had a whole struggle going on—getting that deep, revealing that pain (he had been masking it all his life). It's scary." Pryor worried about how his fans would react, especially his black audience. Would they understand where he was coming from?

"People are going to come in expecting laughs," said Pryor, "and they'll see this different side of me. I don't want to be used to bring in the black audience and then to have them devastated. They have to be prepared. I don't think I could stand the rejection."

Director Schrader said, "Richard can do it all—comedy, romance, drama. He has a boyish quality that allows him to do or say almost anything and be forgiven." Does that mean that Pryor is not dangerous? Is he being seen as a mannish child, loud but cute?

"He can say things no other black man can get away with and a white audience will put up with it because his manner lessens the threat without diluting the message."

Is Schrader saying that Pryor can say the same things as a Malcolm X, or a Martin Luther King, Jr., or a Mudbone, or a Oilwe*eeeelll*, and not get his ass kicked, or his brains blown out, maybe even get paid money for it? And if so, why should white folks be the yardstick by which things are judged? Because they're putting up the money? Or because they are the ones who can snuff a sucker out?

But with all the allowances given to Pryor, Schrader, like many others, predominately white and seasoned with a goodly supply of "upwardly mobile" blacks, feels that Pryor is still not cool enough. Says Schrader, "Richard will be the biggest star in history if he can keep the reins on himself or bite his tongue."

Are they worried that Pryor is putting too much message in his madness rather than method to his magic? Mad because Pryor was not making the folks giggle, blush, and laugh? Was he making folks wiggle and writhe, shift uncomfortably in their seats?

Probably. But what's so bad about that? *Playboy*

said *Blue Collar* was "propaganda, but humanistic and compassionate rather than subversive."

Blue Collar, unlike any Pryor film to that point, marked the direction that Pryor was taking. He had moved black, the black man, his lifestyle, his mannerisms, his problems, into the stream of American life, or at least brought that reality to the screen where it had been sorely ignored and distorted when attempts were made to "do the right thing by the colored American." In *Blue Collar* as Pryor tells it, "The *plant* is just short for plantation."

About the movie, Pryor says, "I'm happy about the outcome; what the story is about in terms of society. It's just a metaphor for life. The consequences are not about what they appear to be but it's everybody's life affects everybody's life—and that part of it was good—in nigger language; It's a Motherfucker!"

In any language Pryor is running down some pretty heavy stuff. And it seemed that he meant it, remembering who he was, what he was about, where he came from.

"Now, baby, look," his grandmother once told him. "You're going up and you can come down a lot faster than you come up, so don't forget where you come from. Peoria is your home, these are your friends around here. Everybody know you went to school around here and I raised you. So don't forget us back here."

Pryor tried not to. "I am successful and make a lot of money but I still have to live as a person, I can't lose my perspective. I know what I am. Black America made me famous."

Baby, if you don't like peaches,
Please don't shake my tree.
If you don't like strawberries,
You better let my bushes be.
                    —The Blues

7

Chapter 7: His Own Nigger

In May of 1977 Richard Pryor took his act back to television, but on his own terms. He had held out, did his thing and proved that he was a very marketable property. On top of that "ethnic" shows were not doing too bad in the ratings game, and that was what the business was all about, ratings.

Gamesmen Pryor and Franklin were up for what television was putting down and Pryor put together an NBC-TV special that sizzled the ratings.

It was really a gamble for NBC-TV which, as the number three horse in a three horse race, was desperate to find something that might overtake ABC-TV's front-running "Happy Days" and "Laverne and Shirley."

But why would they put their money on a wild, unpredictable nigger who just might get their license pulled?

Copycat shows had always worked in the past. Why something as outlandish as Richard Pryor?

The May Special was simply a test. Burt Sugarman, who produced *Midnight Special* for NBC, had worked with Pryor on that show. He knew what Pryor could do. He knew there was an audience.

It was a special like none television had ever seen, at least from a comedian. Red Skelton could make a person misty outside of his humor. Pryor made people cry.

One poetic sequence employed the talents of Maya Angelou who was cursed with a drinking husband. It was a beautiful piece that evolved and grew beyond the tragedy, the bitterness, to something special, love.

A children's group touched heartstrings with an artful interpretation of Stevie Wonder's *Black Man*.

A riotous Pryor introduced Reverend White and his court of pretty women, strutting and talkin' shit, and collecting that money, money, money. And Richard danced for the people.

The Neilsens were hot on it. Pryor was the man! Pryor was good for television. Or at least so they thought. Maybe they hadn't really looked at the show? Maybe it was because they simply didn't account for the curiousity piece attraction the volatile black comedian might have had on a one-shot run. A lot of people had never seen that mouth that could cripple. And everyone was curious as to what a Richard Pryor could and would do if given a full hour of prime time. The worst that could happen would be that he would go up in a rush of blue smoke.

"NBC would love to make me a household word," said Pryor. "They're the number three network and they want to make money and get a good rating off my show's success. But I'm not interested in becoming a household word. I'm interested in my art."

Maybe it was Pryor's parody of big bad black man Idi Amin, who was telling a lot of very sophisticated white people to kiss his ass, that pleased the audience. Maybe they had forgotten that Pryor had once said, on the subject of the portly potentate, "I like Idi Amin because white people hate him so much. The nigger's crazy! But when they try to prove it, he comes out looking sane."

Whatever the case Pryor's attorney, David Franklin, worked out a deal that would net Pryor some $2 million dollars for a prime time series on NBC-TV, restricting Pryor from appearing on any competing networks for five years.

It was a grand moment in television history. Prime time was about to get an X rating. Where was the "Bleeper Brigade?" Or had Pryor toned down? Had he compromised? Had the big dollars been too much for him to ignore?

Compromised? No. Pryor said, "I'd like to get the names of these people who say they're protecting the public by trying to prevent my form of communication. That's a political decision, not a moral one. I want to know why I can't do something. But if it's something I really want I'll fight for it."

Pryor was both attracted and turned-off by television. It was a difficult time and he admitted, "I really don't think TV will ever change."

But it was something he had to do. It was a medium he had not yet conquered. "I don't really want to go around the country playing clubs, seeing cities. I did that already. I have this new house. I want to stay put and do films."

He added television to that list of wants. But it was a

shortlived romance that began with a ten show deal which Pryor sued to have changed to four. "I didn't want to do ten," Pryor said flatly.

Redd Foxx had jumped NBC-TV and *Sanford and Son* went into rerun. NBC-TV went with their big gun. They loaded Pryor and cocked the hammer.

By the time Pryor had gone into production for his series, he and Pam Grier were no longer such a hot item. "We're still close friends," Pryor said, adding, "I'm not a person to do things for publicity. I like being in love. Now there is a very special lady out there who I'm really in love with. It's tough trying to get over her."

It would be hard for anyone to believe that Pryor didn't do things just for the sake of publicity if he hadn't already been labeled as "crazy." People expected Pryor to do the unexpected. They were disappointed when he acted normal.

But who was the mystery woman that Pryor found it "tough trying to get over?" Didn't his bread, his talent, his fame make him a worthy catch for any woman? Who was resisting the Pryor charm?

Before the mystery was solved, Pryor had another surprise up his sleeve. He and the NBC-TV censors were at each others throats and the show had not as yet aired.

What now? Pryor had plopped down $85,000 of his own money, telling attorney Franklin to "write a check" to cover the amount the first show had gone over budget. Isn't that the kind of action one would be glad to see coming from a star? The man was concerned about his show. Maybe too concerned.

The censors were headhunting again. And Pryor wasn't about to back down. "I don't just let people write it and I go out and do it," Pryor said. "I'm involved from day one to the finished product . . . we know what we feel. Then for somebody to tell us that ain't right and they weren't with us and didn't feel our energies and are not working with us, that's just asinine.''

NBC-TV had made the mistake. They let Pryor come on his own terms, never realizing just what Pryor had on his mind, never really seeing Pryor and what he was about. Dazzled by the package they overlooked its contents.

"I think after they got me," said Pryor, "they didn't want me when they realized that I was not going for that okey-doke pressure thing. They wanted to have format and the same old stuff.''

Didn't Pryor know that was the meat and drink of television? That it's medicore predictability was what made it successful? Or at least the audience supposedly reached by teleision was not one that was prone to think, or want to think, or be surprised, but rather simply be entertained. Television had learned that you find out what the people can tolerate and you shove the same thing at them until they just can't take anymore. No one tried to be different all the time. What if the audience didn't laugh one night?

Pryor didn't care. "No, I don't work that way," he said. "I don't feel like that about comedy. I think its sporadic and spontaneous and it should be related that way—from my point of view of black awareness and where I come from and what I see. They couldn't see that. I don't believe they really wanted to. I think if I had done ten shows it would have damaged me mentally.''

Pryor was *thinking*. And while he did not really have a philosophy of comedy, or for that matter life, Pryor was still driven by some very real attitudes that bound him as strongly as any religious code would a fanatic.

That's what he was talking about when he said, "I don't know what I do. I know what I *won't* do. I don't know what I will do." Simple and logical but when put into motion it seems to take on different proportions and dimensions. It seems that it loses a great deal when translated into white folks' ways of saying and doing things. Unfortunately Pryor was not white, or a nigger for that matter. Pryor was speaking a very special language, his own. He was his own nigger for once in his life and nobody was ready for it.

"Usually I don't have any problems unless somebody messes with me," Pryor said. "Then I have problems."

But he knew from jump street what television was all about. Why didn't he see that nothing had changed and stay away? Was it the money?

Partly, Pryor admitted later, " . . . I bit off more than I can chew. I was turning into a greedy person. They give you so much money you can't refuse."

But Pryor did balk, saying to his staff of writers who begged him to hold on, even hiring a plane to fly over pulling a huge banner which read: SURRENDER RICHARD. Pryor agreed to do the four shows and nothing more.

On the eve of the premiere of the first *Richard Pryor Show*, Pryor called a press conference to announce his displeasure with some of the members of the NBC hierarchy.

Displaying a calm that was not reflective of the old Pryor, of the legendary stab-you-with-a-fork temperament, he quietly informed the press gathering that he was not looking for a fight with NBC but refused to be censored.

"They're stifling my creativity," Pryor said, holding

tightly to the hand of a somber-faced beauty who he never introduced to the gathering. The young woman would later prove to be another surprise Pryor had in store for his public.

The furor surrounded Pryor's refusal to edit out or change the opening sequence to his first show. A monologue, the sequence shows Pryor, nude from the waist up, explaining to the viewing audience that he really has his own show. It is no sham.

Pryor explains that most people were sure that he would have to compromise and give up everything in order to be allowed on television, that it was only a joke.

The camera pulls back slowly, and Pryor quips, "Look at me standing here naked." He is wearing a body stocking and looks completely nude. "I haven't given up anything," he says sheepishly and then it is evident that his genitals are not covered but *missing*.

The sequence, initially approved by NBC executives, was later judged offensive by the same executives. They were rattled. They had opened up a Pandora's Box and couldn't shut the lid.

Herminio Traviesas, the head of NBC's Broadcasting Standards Department, with the responsibility of censoring the network's shows, felt that the skit was offensive and could not be aired.

Who was gaming whom? What was so offensive? And who was offended?

Irwin Segelstein, head of programming, approved the skit if the line, "Look at me I'm standing here naked," was edited out.

Did he hope that no one would notice that Pryor was naked, or at least simulated as naked, if he didn't say that he was? What was the problem? He wasn't really naked. He was showing less than the Dallas Cowboys cheerleaders.

Traviesas ruled that the skit could not be aired in any form.

"It's not offensive," Pryor defended. "You've got to have artistic insight. I was making a statement on why I was doing television. They didn't want to offend children at 8 o'clock," Pryor explained.

It hurt. Pryor loves kids. An avid cartoon addict, Pryor had an insight into the kinds of things that television was feeding kids and he knew that the objections to his opening skit were jive. Most probably he had hurt a few feelings because he didn't break into a buck n' wing as soon as the NBC biggies blew hot wind in his direction. Maybe the NBC people should have dug Oscar Brown, Jr., when he crooned, "You knew I was a snake before you took me in."

"It's a violation of artist's rights," Pryor insisted. "It's very hard to work under these conditions. If they're advertising me as being irreverent and outrageous," and the campaign was just that, suggesting that Pryor was going to pull stunts that might well be beyond the realm of the X-rated, "I have a right to be irreverent and outrageous," he said.

"That's what they hired me for. They didn't hire somebody else. They hired Richard Pryor."

There were those who were quick to say that Pryor should have realized that television was a world of illusion. It played tricks with the eyes and the mind. It was like a Disneyland ride through Alice's Wonderland, there just ain't no such place. Sure, the network hired Pryor because his rep was marketable, but when they hired soldiers they didn't expect them to kill anyone, and so they didn't expect that Pryor would really turn out to be all they said he was. That was just the "come on," part of the game of serious "hyping."

Part of the problem was the change in time slot which moved the *Richard Pryor Show* from the adult hour of 10 p.m. to the kiddie hour of 8 p.m. NBC-TV was trying to shoot down the American family hour as presented by front-runner ABC in the form of "Happy Days" and "Laverne and Shirley." It was a bold move trying to use a very black show to challenge the lily white America that was reflected in ABC's offering.

"We were told the opening piece for the first show was objectionable," said David Franklin, "because it airs at 8 p.m., when a lot of children are watching. But NBC decided on the time slot. We didn't care when the show was put on. At first we were scheduled on a different night at around 10 p.m."

Pryor called the press conference and made his stance because he didn't want people to think that he was "just another nigger who ran off from NBC."

It was something that Pryor really did not want to do. He knew the power of television. He knew the impact his art would have, the truth would have, if allowed to be aired.

"It," Pryor said, "could be such an informative medium. One week of truth on TV could just straighten out everything. One hundred and twenty-seven million people watch television every night, that's why they use it to sell stuff. They've misused it a long time so now it's just a business . . . It's just a place where you sell products."

The NBC censors held their ground and Pryor wouldn't give in. "If the censors tamper with this show," Franklin said, "then he would well throw down the gauntlet."

To no one's astonishment the *Richard Pryor Show* premiered on a Tuesday night with the controversial scene deleted. Most of America had already gotten its fill of the skit during the nightly news—on all the networks.

The sequence that caused all the trouble was tame in comparison to the rest of the show. "Nigger" was part of the Pryor language and it was used often and off-handedly throughout the show. But the censors did not seem concerned about the ministers, lawyers, doctors, teachers of middle class black America who bristled when it was used. It was obscene. Black folks wanted the word banned but the NBC censors didn't seem to care.

"Pryor retaliated," said David Felton, "with a manuever that should earn him a place in the *Guiness Book of Poetic Justice*. He gave NBC four hours that were so bizarre and puzzling that the network had no way of censoring them, because no one knew what the fuck was going on."

It was Pryor at his wildest, attacking everything that was American or dear to the hearts of Americans. He had rough and tumble cowboys facing off. "Next time we gonna kill yo' ass!" countered by, "My donkey don't like to be called ass."

A steel worker, the hard hat symbol of American macho, was featured in a skit singing, "I've got to be me," while stepping out of his closet *and* his clothes to reveal a me that was on the top of Anita Bryant's Hit List.

Pryor had taken people beyond tongue and cheek. He wasn't hiding anything. He was saying openly, "Look here America, this here is what *we* all are about. Ain't it some shit? Funny and otherwise. But it's us."

156

As an evangelist with a Rastaman hairdo, Pryor, for the first time on national television, has his feet kissed by not one, but *two* white women. They canned Sammy Davis, Jr., for standing too close to one of them on stage.

For the first, and possibly the last time on national television, a black man grabbed two white women (Siamese twins) in a very sexually suggestive manner and advised—in answer to their, "We never have any fun"—that they should try sex. He immediately offered his help and threw his own hips into a gyrating frenzy. Where were the censors? The nigger had lost his mind.

For the first time on national television, which has perpetuated the myth that more is better when speaking of women's breasts, a black man reached out with his boney, grasping fingers and grabbed the ample mounds of a white woman. Where was the Klan?

In another scene Pryor poses as a wild rock star who tantalizes the kids with dope and drugs and then sprays them with machine guns and pills and gas, screaming, "I'll kill ya." There was nothing funny but it was very, chillingly real. There were no black kids in the group that was wasted by the "Black Death" image.

A San Francisco TV columnist called the material "black racist." Black people rejected Pryor's free use of the word nigger. The shows did not overthrow the dynasty of *Happy Days* and *Laverne and Shirley*. NBC was off the hook.

While the show did poorly in the ratings it is clear that NBC did little to insure success. Pryor clearly was never suited for the 8 p.m. slot, not because he would have offended children, but because most of America, including many black Americans, were not ready for what Pryor was trying to tell them. The Fonz was as far out as

Americans wanted to get, at least in their illusions. The Fonz was simply an urban version of The Duke. Pryor was a nigger. A dangerous nigger.

"I don't want to be on TV," Pryor said in desperation. "I'm in a trap. I can't do this—there ain't no art." He cried, but he didn't relent. "I'm gonna have to be ruthless here," he told his staff, "because of what it does to my life. I'm not stable enough. I don't want to drink and I don't want to snort and I can't do it no other way."

While NBC announced that Pryor's show failed because of low ratings, the truth was that NBC had bitten off more than they could chew and were looking for a scapegoat. Pryor had already gained enough bad press to fit that bill perfectly.

In a *Players* magazine interview, comic/actor Scoey Mitchell charged, "Nobody is probing and bugging NBC to find out why Richard Pryor's show didn't work. And here is a man who is a comedic genius and his show was sabotaged over there at NBC. But the black press was more interested in him shooting a gun up in the air. (Mitchell is referring to a Pryor incident that took place in the early hours of a new year.)

Pryor took his "Blackjack" routine to television and the execs hid their eyes and didn't laugh. They didn't want to see that kind of shit.

In typical Pryor fashion he walked onto the set of his TV show and introduced as his brand new wife model/actress Deboragh McGuire, the beauty who had stood silently next to Pryor, holding his hand throughout the press conference.

It seemed that Pryor had finally fulfilled himself. He had stood his ground, made some money and finally married the sweetheart he had longed for. It was mutual, McGuire said, "I'm still in shock. It's unbeliev-able . . . I got him."

The mystery was broken, McGuire was that "very special lady" who he was "really in love with."

Pryor had confessed his love to a *Jet* writer and it was reported. After the story appeared, Pryor said, "She called me. It was like a drum beat going out. I told her that we couldn't go on any longer the way we had been and that we had to get married."

The newlyweds had had an on-again-off-again rela-tionship which had been going on for about four years. But it looked as if all that was in the past. Fans hoped that Deboragh McGuire Pryor would prove to be that stabilizing force that Pryor seemed to need so desper-ately.

The couple was married in a private ceremony of close friends and family members at Pryor's Northridge home. Pryor was still keeping his "real stuff" out of the public eye. Rev. Austin S. Williams officiated.

In less than a week's time Pryor showed his backside to the world again. He hadn't changed at all. Wedded bliss had not tamed the savage breast. Maybe Pryor just couldn't be tamed. Or maybe it was still part of some elaborate game he was running on the world. This time Pryor loosed a staggering volley against the gay com-munity.

Invited to appear at a benefit and rally sponsored by a Gay Rights organization which was billed as a "human rights rally," Pryor accepted. He was all for the fight for rights. A great many of his had been stepped on. The evening, attended by the brightest stars in Holly-wood, Levar Burton, Paul Newman, Lily Tomlin, Bette Midler, Helen Reddy, Valerie Harper and more, took an unexpected turn and ended in bedlam.

"Kiss my happy, rich, black ass!" challenged Pryor before stomping off the stage of the Hollywood Bowl where the rally was held. And he wasn't kidding. He was mad and meant what he said.

The Gay Rights group was shocked. Was Pryor just proving his reputation? Was he drunk? Loaded? What had the gays done to him?

Aaron Russo, Bette Midler's concert producer, put the rally together and explained Pryor's actions, saying, "I like controversy as much as anyone but there is a time and a place for it. This was a night for human rights," Russo went on, "with a special emphasis for gay rights. I think he went so far because he found himself bombing on stage after he got the first few laughs."

Pryor bombing on stage? Impossible. Not the Pryor who was the King of the improv. Not the Richard Pryor who could take two words—"I feel"—and create another world with intonation alone. How could he bomb? His eyes, his face, his voice, all he had to do was stand there and he would have been funny.

In self-defense, knowing that he would never get a fair shake from the white press—17,000 gays couldn't be wrong, especially if they could blow $50 a piece for the rally—Pryor put in a phone call to Jim Cleaver, the executive editor of the Los Angeles *Sentinel*, a black weekly newspaper.

"I was invited there under the pretext of a human rights rally," said Pryor. "But it was not . . . It was a gay rights rally and that is what they should have called it."

Officially the rally was hawked as a "Star-Spangled Night For Rights: A Celebration For Human Rights." But the bread was going to a San Francisco-based gay educational organization Save Our Human Rights

160

Foundation, Inc. The evening was more of an attack on the Anita Bryants of the world than a celebration of Human Rights.

Pryor told Cleaver that his jaws first got tight when he saw that a black dance group, The Lockers, wasn't being treated the same as the white groups.

"When a white dance act went on stage," said Pryor, "every damn body and his brother went to fix the lights. They didn't do shit for The Lockers."

"Then a fire marshal started to reprimand a black youngster," Pryor told Cleaver, "and all the white folks simply turned their backs and ignored what was going on and I got mad as hell."

Pryor's spokesman called it a race thing, saying Pryor's outburst had nothing to do with any anti-gay feelings on Pryor's part.

During the course of his brief appearance, before he "went off" on the audience, Pryor had explained that he had once had a gay experience, but at that time it was called "fucking a faggot."

It set the tone for what Pryor was to say next. "I came here for human rights," he roared, "but I am *seeing* what it's really about.

"Fags are prejudiced," Pryor charged. "I see the four niggahs you have dispersed. White folks are having good fun here tonight. The Locker Dancers came back stage dripping with sweat but all you could say is 'Oh that was nice.' But when the ballet dancers came out dancing to that funny music you said, 'Wow, those are some bad mothers' . . ."

The audience was at a loss. Were they supposed to laugh? Was there a joke somewhere that they were missing?

Maybe he was kidding. Everyone had heard Pryor's

routine: "White folks don't give a nigger a break. Jackson Five be singing their asses off and they be talking about the Osmond Brothers. Fuck the Osmond Brothers!"

Had he forgotten his lines? Was he trying to improvise because he forgot how the piece was supposed to go?

Pryor was serious. And he left no doubt about that. "Anita's getting over," he said. "How can fags be racists? I thought since this was a night for human rights, there'd be some human beings here.

"This is an evening about human rights," Pryor said, "and I'm a human being. I just wanted to see where you was *really* at, and I wanted to test you to your mother-fucking *soul*. I'm doing this shit for *nuthin'*. But I wanted to come here and tell you to kiss my ass . . . with your bullshit. You understand?

"Kiss my happy, rich black ass!" he stormed and then left the stage. This time he wasn't questioning himself like he did the night he walked off the stage in the Alladin Hotel. He wasn't asking, "What the fuck am I doing here?" He knew what the hell he came to do, and he knew what he had to do when he found out what was going down. And he did it. Wasn't it expected of him? That quick temper? Brashness?

Lily Tomlin said it all. "When you hire Richard Pryor, you get Richard Pryor."

While there are those who would say that Pryor is paranoid, jousting with windmills, there are just as many who would celebrate him for "not taking any shit!"

"They called it a human rights rally," Pryor complained to the *Sentinel*. "But that didn't have nuthin' to do with human rights. What about that little girl who

162

died in Chicago because they wouldn't accept her at the hospital? Hell, that is *human* rights."

Newsweek was impressed enough with Pryor's antics to run a Maureen Oth article, "The Perils of Pryor." He had made the big time. He was making very *big* waves.

For some it would have been the perfect set up for kicking back and enjoying the California sun. He had his soulmate Deboragh, lucrative contracts for films with Universal and Warner Brothers Studios, the sharpest lawyer on the set in David Franklin, and more money than he could count. What more could he want? Why wouldn't he settle down?

A young Freddie Prinz said, "He's the best, he's the goddamn best . . . Man, Pryor knows what's right; he's paid all the dues. If I could get five minutes like any of his stuff, I'd *come* for months."

The rooster and the chicken had a fight
The chicken kick the rooster out of sight;
The rooster told the chicken, "That's all right -
I'll see you in the gumbo tomorrow night."

Chapter 8: Bad Nigger!

On November 9, 1977, Richard Pryor was visiting with his grandmother, Mrs. Marie Carter Pryor Bryant, in Peoria, Illinois, when he collapsed from intense chest pains. The comic was rushed to the hospital.

On November 10, 1977, the country was stunned by reports that Richard Pryor, acid-tongued Crazy Nigger, was dead! Tongues wagged. Everyone knew what happened. The nigger self-destructed. Snorted up too much of that white stuff and blew his brains out. Whites and blacks alike accepted and reported death. It all fit. It was the way that Richard Pryor would want to go, at home, with his grandmother nearby. The perfect end to a tortured life. Finally he had found peace and security. Somewhere over Jordan.

It was a shortlived rumor. The truth came out. And

the tongue-waggers argued that if the nigger wasn't dead, he damn sure should've been dead. All that booze and dope. It was a wonder he hadn't killed himself long before.

Maybe Pryor heard his detractors, those fans who would miss him, and those who wouldn't. And maybe he didn't like what he heard. Maybe he knew that if he died at that moment he would never rest quietly in his grave because very few people would really know why he had lived. Maybe his work wasn't finished. Or maybe it was just wishful thinking on the part of those who initiated the rumor. Pryor did not die.

His grandmother said that he had had a mild heart attack and had been driven to the hospital in a private car and walked into the hospital under his own power.

Pryor ordered the doctors at Methodist Medical Center in Peoria, where he was taken, to keep quiet about his condition. Pryor was still holding on very tightly to his "real stuff."

Bill Cosby became the 1690th celebrity to be honored with a star on Hollywood's great walk of fame, and Pryor had been presented with a premature tomb stone. It was a preview of things to come for Pryor. He just didn't know how hard the rain was going to fall.

His film *Which Way Is Up*? was making big money at the box office. Brought in for a low $3 million dollar budget, *Which Way Is Up*? had reaped a healthy $15 million in domestic and Canadian rentals and between $8 million and $9 million in foreign rentals.

It was too early for Pryor to drop off the set. There was still money to be made and there was no substitute. For good or ill there was only one Richard Pryor.

"I believe in the spirit of living," said Pryor in December of 1977. "It's just good to be alive. If you're alive then you always have the potential to change things. I care about living life. Sometimes it's better to have nothing, then you don't have to worry about trying to go out and spend a lot of money.''

What could go wrong? He was off drugs, or at least he had said he was. He was married. He had money. *Jet* magazine reported that December of 1977 was Richard Pryor's "Richest Xmas." And a film on the life of Charlie Parker still had not been released.

"Pryor was ready to be fully exposed this year," David Franklin told *Jet*, "and quite frankly I was ready too. He is the biggest black star in Hollywood today and by all means this is his richest Christmas."

Pryor said: "I'm a little embarrassed by it all. I guess it has been one of my richest Christmases. But I call this my harvest year. I planted the crop for what happened this year 17 years ago. I'm just beginning to reap the harvest.

"Every year I start off the season mad," Pryor said, "about what has happened to Christmas and then there I am with my mouth stuck out if I don't get a gift. And there I am on Christmas Eve doing Christmas shopping."

But Pryor was a realist. He came from the streets and he knew that life was no crystal palace. Especially not for a black man who still had the taste of nigger on his breath.

"Life is a struggle," Pryor said, and recognized that "happiness comes very seldom. You get a little bit here and a little bit there. Most of it is a fight. That anybody lives is a miracle."

Pryor ended the old year and brought in the New Year on a sour note. He didn't "start off the season mad" he ended it that way, after emptying a big bore

.357 magnum pistol into a Buick that he had already rammed with his own Mercedes Benz. When the news picked it up, everyone knew what had happened and why. The tongue waggers and clickers were burning up the wires. Pryor had finally flipped out completely. Drugs and booze had taken their toll on his brain cells. Maybe blood quit pumping to his brain when he had had the heart attack in Peoria.

The smoke was still belching from the barrel of the .357 when Deboragh McGuire Pryor hit her husband of four months with a divorce suit. Was this the same woman that Pryor had a "nose job" behind? He once said, "It's tough trying to get over her."

Close observers suggested that the relationship had never really been all that stable. Still, it was another jolt to Pryor's faithful fans who were running out of excuses for the brother. Would he eventually kill somebody?

Deboragh McGuire Pryor sought $2,480 a month in ailimony payments, stating that Mr. Pryor earned about $50,000 a month and was worth more than a million dollars.

Singer-dancer Beverly Clayborn filed suit in Los Angeles Superior Court on January 19 for $17 million. Miss Clayborn alleged that Pryor made an "unprovoked attack," on her person and caused her to be injured in her "physical and mental well being." Miss Clayborn wore a neck brace when she appeared in court. She was in the Buick which became victim to Pryor's wrath.

Pryor said, "If she gets it (the $17 million), I'll marry her."

Edna Solomon, Miss Clayburn's sister, was also present in Pryor's Northridge home when he went off. The two women asserted that they had been guests in the

Pryor home as friends of Pryor's bride when Pryor suddenly yelled, "I'll give you bull-dykin' bitches five seconds to get out of my house!"

The women said that they ran outside and locked themselves in their car when Pryor started counting. Allegedly Pryor then rammed their car "seven times" with his Mercedes Benz.

Judge Morton Rochman presided over the case and ordered that the felony charge for assault with a gun be dropped, while maintaining charges of felony assault with a deadly weapon (his car) and a misdemeanor count of malicious mischief.

Lawyer David Franklin flew in from Atlanta to see that his client was getting a fair shake. It looked like Pryor had finally gone too far with his jive. His record of violence was more than legend now.

In April of 1978, Pryor decided that he had better "tell it all." *Jet* magazine's Bob Lucas provided a sensitive ear for the comic's story.

"I mess up a great deal in my life," Pryor began, comforted by the security provided by his Northridge mansion. " . . . I've never hurt anybody in all the bullshit I do.

"My biggest problem was drinking and snorting cocaine," he admitted. "That's the only time I get in trouble . . . But I no longer have fun with it and I don't want to self-destruct myself."

What was he running from? Why did he hide in drugs and booze?

Pryor said that his problems "stem from the fact that I have a lot of guilt about being successful. I'm not able to deal with the success that I have. And I have a lot of pressures. It's not about the big head or nuthin' like that, it's about my life.

171

"Life doesn't change when you start making money," Pryor said. "You have the same problems you've always had."

There are those who would argue that Pryor was crazy. But they are the type who will never have the opportunity to prove him wrong.

More and more Pryor was forced to talk about his "real stuff." His personal life had always been a tightly kept secret. It pained him to have his business blared at so openly. Especially when white people were involved.

Pryor told Lucas: "I hate the fact that this black woman pointed at me in court. That hurt me more than anything. The white man asked, 'Who is it?' ain't nobody else but me there. I'd rather stood up myself and said, 'I did it. Y'all don't have to point at me' "

They had treed the rebel. They were jeering at him and Pryor could not stand the pressure—it was crippling.

"It's just degrading, humiliating," Pryor said, "to have the white man be able to talk to me . . . period. Other than: Mr. Pryor, can I get out of your way?' or 'Here's your money!' "

Pryor was cut deeply, "When I do something that is especially involved with black people, regardless of the circumstances—which I don't want to discuss—it hurts me to my heart because black people have made me rich and famous."

But he knew that he had to talk about those situations no matter how painful, he could not hold back. "I really meant those women no harm," he explained, "other than to scare them for what they did to me. (Pryor has a simple policy. Don't fuck with him and he won't fuck with you.)

"Here's what I would like to say about what happened New Years," Pryor started, the flood gates opening so that he might purge himself of the excess pain. "It was beween my wife and I, and I don't figure her friends have no business jumping in it no more than my friends have any business jumping in. That's between me and my wife . . .

If you see me and my wife fighting in the middle of Sunset Boulevard," Pryor went on, "drive around us or over us, but don't get out of the car and start messing with us . . . if you add on to it, it's just gonna get bigger and bigger."

And his ex-wife? "I love my wife very much," he said. "When she tells me something I believe it. I don't want people to think (anything bad) about her. She's a fine person, a good human being, plus she's gonna be rich when we divorce.

"I'm not competing to be the one who's married the most in Hollywood. Every woman I ever married, I've loved them, the white ones, the black ones, all of them, I've loved them . . . my women."

Deboragh was Pryor's first legal wife, and his second black wife. His first three "wives" were married without benefit of clergy or legality. He would later tell Barbara Walters in a nationally televised interview, "I married one person. I married Deboragh."

While Pryor was repentant, he was by no means walking with his tail tucked between his legs. "Now, I ain't gonna be no funny ass nigger," he said, "and change my life completely. I will fool around and have big fun. But that other shit (drugs), I have left alone."

Was he jiving? Was he looking for sympathy? Was he using that lost dog, little boy charm that allowed him to say anything he wanted to find favor with the masses? Was he afraid that he had gone too far with his bullshit?

173

He told David Felton of *Rolling Stone*, things went wrong, "maybe because I was immature, or maybe because it wasn't right. You write your own script."

How long could Pryor continue to "write his own script?" Times had changed. The American public did not want to hear about "negative things or negative people." People wanted to get over, to make it. Things were tough all over. People wanted to indulge themselves, laugh, be happy.

The press jumped on him. The words were not good. Pryor had pissed off all the blacks who had hoped that he would prove to be a "credit to the race." Cosby had. He was peddling Del Monte products and Jello and Fords. Pryor couldn't peddle cocaine. He was his own worst enemy.

Cosby got the message, saying, "In this country, business is conducted on their (corporate white executives') own ground. In this country business is conducted in white English. You don't 'get down' when talking with the chairman of the board. You don't punctuate every sentence with a 'right on!'—not unless you want to be right out . . . on your ass."

Is that where Pryor was headed? Out on his ass? If a few 'right ons' would upset a corporate exec, a heavy dose of Pryor's "niggers" and "motherfuckers" would drive an exec right out a window. What could Pryor do to save himself?

First he had to beat the rap that might promise him some jail time. His fans might forgive but the law is the law, and Pryor knew from first hand experience that the law did not jive. His ass was in a serious sling.

But Pryor is a resilient brother. He always seems to spring back stronger than ever from all the crises that have faced him. It's almost as if he grows stronger more ominous with each downfall, thriving on chaos.

"My uncle taught me this," Pryor said, " 'The thing to do is, you go and take some time for yourself, and you review your whole life. You look at everything that you've ever done, or ever thought. And you don't deny no thoughts, and you don't deny no actions you ever committed. And you see who you are.'

"The good, the bad, the horrifying and all that shit— you look at it, square in the face. It's kinda like purging yourself—cleaning out, facing them demons and wiping 'em out."

Pryor was a man surrounded by demons, or so he thought, afraid even to really relax outside of his North-ridge home. Or was it paranoia that prompted him to say, "People tell me, 'you ought to just lie on the beach and close your eyes.' I can't do that. I gotta keep one eye open out of fear that somebody is gonna sneak up and hit me with a board."

He was right to be so cautious. His future would hold more and more attacks from the black middle class who were tired of his niggerish antics at a time when black kids needed powerful role models.

Pryor was never one to try to "put on" for other folks, black or white. He wasn't about to reform. He had been asked to speak to children on the subject of drugs and refused. "I feel like a hypocrite," Pryor explained. "As much cocaine as I snorted. The kids know that; they ain't stupid. All I can say to kids is, 'Know what you want to do.' I can tell them there ain't nothing happening in jail. You'll die, or be treated like a dog. If that's what they want, fine. I can't stop it."

That's not what middle class black America wanted to hear. And weren't they the ones who had the bread to spend on Pryor concerts and albums and films?

Shouldn't he listen to their pleas? What harm was there in their protecting their children from the horrors of life, from the "niggerness" that white people would coat and cripple them with?

No harm at all, probably. But it isn't the way Pryor plays the game. He plays it straight. There is only one way for him, the truth is the supreme knowledge, the superior weapon, he brandishes it and clings to it with a passion, no matter who, or how deeply, it hurts.

Pryor would tell Felton, "You know, I felt it was over. I was splintered . . . in many pieces, right? And it was just all—actually, I felt relieved." Felton says Pryor begins to laugh. "To tell the truth," he went on, "now that I think about it, I felt relieved. And then my life was my own again. I had a chance to do what I really love."

And what did Pryor really love? He said he really loved Deboragh. But the truth is, Pryor is probably not capable of loving anything or anyone as much as he loves his work, his art.

He's given up so much for it, money, part of his sanity. Maybe he is incapable of giving that kind of devotion on a one-to-one basis. Maybe through his art he finds a means of communicating his large need to love and be loved to the world, a suitable lover.

He cared enough about the quality of his work over quantity by submitting An Open Letter To Members of NARAS after being notified that he was being considered for a Grammy award for one of his albums.

The letter read:

"When I recently received notification that I had been voted a Grammy nomination by the members of NARAS I was, and I continue to be, appreciative of the recognition given to me. I would like to publicly thank

NARAS for this nomination.

"My appreciation of the honor of this nomination is, however, tainted by my knowledge that the material under consideration was recorded 10 years ago and recently re-packaged and released.

"My appreciation of the honor you have given me with your nomination is real. My unwillingness to have 10 year old material up for consideration is just as real. Therefore, I intend to cast my vote for one of the other nominees, and I urge you to do the same."

No one can show any more self-destructive tendencies than someone who is putting *himself* down. What difference did it make how old the material was, as long as it was his?

That was part of the game in Hollywood. No one ever got anything for what they deserved to get it for. Poitier got an "Oscar" for *Lilies of the Fields*. He should've gotten it for his role opposite Tony Curtis in *The Defiant Ones*.

Liza Minelli missed the gold statuette for *Sterile Cukoo* and hit gold with *Cabaret*. *Sterile Cuckoo* was the more deserving of the two films.

Pryor was too serious about his work to have second rate material pass for what he was about. He had grown. His material should reflect those changes, that growth, that knowledge. "Even Mudbone changes," Pryor said, and, "I like to do that 'cause I figure if you pay new money, you should see a new show."

What could Pryor come up with that was new? Hadn't he blasphemed? Been treasonous in his speech? Racist? Sexist? Anti-gay? What else could he come up with that would top what he had already done?

It seemed that it was all over. The smart money was against Pryor's pulling himself out of the shit he had jumped into. Bad publicity was about to blow him away. Even David M. Franklin wasn't going to be able to save him from doing some serious slammer time.

"Bad publicity can hurt you," Pryor said. "Bad publicity can hurt anybody. But the strong survive. You always look adversity in the face and you turn it around. And you always be truthful. If you tell the truth, can't nobody turn against you. Now, if I lied and tried to skate around something, people would pinpoint me: 'Aw, the nigger's full of shit.''"

Some people say that I'm dead,
But it's all a big mistake,
Some say they were at my funeral,
Some say they were at my wake . . .
The Blues

Chapter 9: Wanted Nigger!

"Rumors of my death," said humorist Mark Twain, "are greatly exaggerated."

The same can be said of the life and career of Richard Pryor who, like Twain, had been prematurely reported dead. Even his career had been assumed to have come to an abrupt end.

But Pryor is made of sterner stuff than most people. And most people were not really prepared for the startling recovery Pryor made as far as his career and image were concerned. It was the work of pure genius.

"Pay-or-play" causes in Pryor's contracts assured him of being paid for his film projects whether the film-makers got the movies together on time or not. Pryor, at least on paper, was still someone special.

Finally, after much dickering and coaxing, Pryor was

able to lure the noted actress Cicely Tyson into working with him on a picture. It was a major break-through for Pryor. He would be playing opposite one of the classiest black actresses in the business.

"Like you need pain to be funny," Pryor once said. 1978 proved to be a painful year for Pryor even though it seemed that he was fighting to come to grips with his life, his career. It looked as if he was facing those "monsters" that haunted him, tripping him up.

Pryor had, for the second time in his life, talked himself out of going to jail. Earlier in his life and career, Pryor faced a Philadelphia magistrate on charges of woman beating. The judge, after seeing Pryor perform, released the comedian with a fine, "because he was too talented to be in jail."

Van Nuys (Calif.) Superior Court Commissioner Sherman Juster had decreed that Pryor's punishment for his misdeeds of New Year's Eve should fit his crime. Pryor had "acted the nigger" that night—who else would pump .357 magnum slugs into a $7,000 Buick?—and Juster ordered that Pryor stage ten charitable concerts as his penalty.

Like any genius, Pryor turned what seemed failure into the most successful album and concert tour of his career. He recaptured his old audience, silenced a few detractors and tongue waggers, pulled in a few new admirers to his cult of laughter and pain, and all-in-all blew everybody's mind with *Wanted*.

It was his masterpiece. A portrait of Richard Pryor at his best. And this time it was Richard Pryor. He wiped away some of the mystique that had surrounded him and stepped forward, sheepishly, naked to the world and said simply: "I really mean I'm happy to see people come out, especially after all the shit I been in." Pryor's voice was soft, repentent, anxious. He didn't storm out on the stage firing barbed insults, he tip-toed out before live audiences in three major cities, tough nuts—New York City, Washington, D.C., and Chicago.

The audience laughs, uncomfortably at first, a few ripples that are like small ridges in an otherwise calm lake.

"I mean it from my heart," Pryor says humbly. "It makes me feel good, as a person . . . it makes me say 'The shit wasn't *that* bad.' All I did was kill a car."

Pryor has got his innocent voice fronting for him. He was feeling the people out. They had come to see him but were they ready for the *real* Richard Pryor.

"You'd think I'd murdered somebody!"

He had them. The audience went wild. They agreed. No, it really wasn't all that bad. Pryor's boyish quality is in control of the audience. He is milking them for sympathy, for understanding. They go for it. Maybe Pryor has changed.

"I thought it was fair," Pryor explains. He's going to talk to them about it, take them into his confidence. "My wife was gonna leave me." The audience applauds. They understand. Anybody would be a little upset.

"But not in *this* motherfucker you ain't," Pryor snorted. "I'm killing this here . . . I had a magnum too, man . . . (the audience is ready—Pryor's about to get real funny) . . . I shot one of them tires—*Booooom* (he groans and moans like a dying tire) . . . it got good to me so I shot another one—*booooom*—(more dying tire noises).

The audience is loose now. They know that Richard has only done what they would have done. What seemed so, so, ah, savage and vicious, when examined in the

183

proper light, didn't really seem so bad after all.

"That vodka I was drinking," Pryor continues, "told me, 'Go on, shoot something else . . . , I shot the motor—the motor fell out the motherfucker! Motor say, 'Fuck it!' "

The group is out of control. Motors don't talk, they know that. But if they did they would have said, "Fuck it!" the same way that Pryor had said it. They were sure of that.

"Then the police came," Pryor is moving, setting the pace. (Innocently) I went into the house . . . They got magnums too . . . and they don't shoot cars. They shoot nig*gaaars*."

And on the police: "I didn't know it was a death penalty for a traffic ticket."

He was painting clear cut images, "and the nigger was low-running, doing an 8.9 hundred through the underbrush."

The audience was responsive. Pryor takes liberties, he's still the same old Pryor. He won't let them forget it.

"Take the picture, nigger," he yells at a member of the audience, then "You ain't got no flash, motherfucker." Then to the audience, signifying like the infamous monkey, "nigger taking pictures his ass off—ain't nuthin' workin'—probably got no film in the motherfucker."

And to another victim in the audience: "Nigger still wearing a dashiki. I know he's crazy. Don't need to fuck with him at all."

Women aren't scared either: "What happened to the hair on my chest? I ain't never had no hair on my chest!" He pauses, "What happened to your pussy?"

It is still early in the performance and Pryor has the audience in the palm of his hand. They are laughing.

They're faces beet red, at least the white folks who have "come back to their seats and find niggers in them," have changed colors.

Pryor wastes no time in letting the audience, black and white, know where he is coming from, what he is standing for.

"My God," Pryor opines. "White people? You motherfuckers came anyway."

The air is cleared away. At least some of the debris is cleared away, some of the doubts, questions, and everyone knows that the air is blue, deep blue with pain, dirty blue with raunch. Pryor is Pryor, nothing's changed. And just maybe, the innocence he seemed to show was part of a game.

Game or no game, it was a painfully funny experience, Pryor had followed his uncle's advice, "The good, the bad, the horrifying and all that shit—you look at it, square in the face."

The people who had made Pryor infamous, Mudbone, Oilwe*ellll*, the young junkie, they were given the night off. Pryor was no longer wearing their masks, speaking through them. *Wanted*, Pryor live, is Pryor being Richard Pryor.

And why not? He had lived long enough, paid enough dues. He was no longer one who simply observed life as experienced by others. He had a very real life of his own. Chaotic at times, yes, but still life. And he had learned to extract from the chaos the precious "knowledge" that helped to explain some of the madness, lessen the pain of living.

The heart attack that he had sloughed off as being nothing more than a bad case of indigestion became one of Pryor's best pieces. It finds its power in its simplicity. It is the tale told without pretentious trappings that disguises false information as truth, misleading for ego's sake. Ego ain't invited to this party.

Mel Brooks once said, "Pryor is the least vain person I know. He hasn't a vain bone in his body."

Wanted justifies the comment. Pryor tells it like it is, using himself and his own shortcomings as a basis for ridicule, as object lesson.

The heart attack sequence tells it all.

"Motherfucker never admits that they ever had a heart attack," says Pryor, his voice quickly changes, very proper, " 'No sir, I never did—I had indigestion once.'

"Them motherfuckers *huurrt*! I was walkin' in the yard and somethin' say, 'Don't breathe no more!' " (The voice is husky, intimidating, his Jesse voice— power to victim.) "I say, 'huh?' ' (the power commands). "Don't breathe no motherfuckin' more—you heard me!'

(The victim whines), "Okay. Okay. I won't breathe. I won't breathe."

(Power storms), "Shut the fuck up! You thinkin' 'bout dyin', ain'tcha nigger?"

"Yeah, yeah, yeah!" (victim whines).

"Why didn't you think about it when you was eatin' that pork, nigger, drinkin' that whiskey and snortin' that cocaine, nigger?"

(Victim moans, grovels), " 'I'm thinkin' 'bout it, I'm thinkin' 'bout it.'

"You put in an emergency call to God."

It's an allegory. It has many meanings beyond the sheer truth of how badly we treat our bodies, realizing how much damage we have done, only when it's too late, and false bravado is quickly replaced by a chilling realization. Man is very, very small, all things considered, and fragile too.

The Heart Attack routine reminds us of Pryor's admission to his excessive use of cocaine, "I snorted up Peru . . . with my dumb self." He is facing his own demons again. And he is allowing his audience to face theirs' through him.

The power of the live performances encouraged pro-motor Bill Sargent to film the Pryor concert and release it as a movie for SEE Theatre Network. Sargent would later admit that *Live In Concert* was "outgrossing *Superman.*"

Impossible. The hero of America upstaged by a skinny nigger from Peoria? No way!

The film was also packaged as a video cassette and re-leased to the public. Pryor had found a better way of beating the television game. It was better than working for NBC. He had finally beaten the censors.

Pryor proved himself to be a reformed citizen, too. And in late 1979, after Pryor had completed five of the ten charitable concerts he had been court-ordered to perform, Court Commissioner Sherman Juster, who had set the punishment, decided that Pryor had suffered enough. The remaining five concerts were dropped.

While Pryor was not burdened by charitable concerts, he did set out on a 22 city tour that set records. Every-one was crowding in to see what the nigger was up to.

He was a hit. Pryor broke Steve Martin's one-night attendance record at the Golden Hall in San Diego and also set a new week attendance record at the Circle Star Theater in San Carlos, California.

In Washington, D.C., after performing four sold-out concerts at the Kennedy Center, Pryor returned to put on his act in the 20,000 seat Capitol Center in order to satisfy ticket demands.

It wasn't enough to make Pryor completely acceptable to the growing population of blacks whose identity crises were based on some need to find a singular definition for the millions of black folk in the country. It was a trying time for Pryor; the abrasive word, "nigger," was *still* souring some of his audience.

Black America was just waking up to the fact that nothing much had changed since the sizzling sixties. They were distraught, fighting shadows that bested them at every turn, even though people like Pryor were trying to cast enough light on things so as to render the shadows powerless. *Nigger* had to go!

There was a minor flap in the black press about "image," and "race pride" and "helping racists" and such, a replay of the early days of the black press when a lot of space was given to chastising those "loud, uncouth members of the race who make noise on public conveyances, wear indecent clothing, and generally give the race a bad name."

It would escalate into much more, further pointing up the identity and image crisis faced by black Americans, as Pryor expanded his comedic form and took on a slapstick role opposite America's favorite, Cool Cos, in Neil Simon's *California Suite*.

Cool Cos doing something to degrade blacks? Not really! That was like saying Cinderella shot smack. What the hell was going on? Had Pryor's racist madness overwhelmed the gentle humorist?

The trouble originated with a review of *California Suite* by *New Yorker* magazine film critic Pauline Kael. She attacked, observing that the actions of Pryor and Cosby "seem to be saying that the men may be doctors but they're still uncontrollable dumb blacks who don't belong in a rich, civilized atmosphere; and the recessive whitened decor turns them into tar babies.''

Kael wasn't kidding. Here was a white woman who was carrying the banner for black identity. It was the same old stuff really, blacks weren't buffoons and concerned folk weren't going to tolerate blacks in those kinds of roles.

On the surface of things it seemed that Kael was on target. It was about time somebody had the guts to call a ''spade'' a spade.

''When they don't know how to handle cars, when they stumble around a flooded room, crash into each other, step on broken glass, or, even worse, when Cosby bites Pryor's nose, it all has horrifying racist overtones . . . *California Suite* would seem to give offense to just about everyone: it goes from confirming the stereotypes of repressed, glamorously unhappy WASPs to confirming the comic stereotypes of henpecked baggie-pants Jews and of blacks who act like clowning savages . . .''

Kael was putting down some serious stuff. And it struck a very sour chord with Cosby and Pryor who had stretched out in their roles in *California Suite* to incorporate a little of that physical, slapstick stuff that worked well for Laurel and Hardy, Abbott and Costello, Dean Martin and Jerry Lewis. What the two comedians didn't know is that it wasn't allowed!

Racism had turned a flip-flop and was cutting with both sides of the blade. The Constitution had said that black folks were as good as everybody else. That countered all the Jim Crow garbage, the absurdities, that justified slavery and segregation. But no one was ever *treated* for their cases of racism and because people had decided to ignore color as the answer to racism, color stepped forward and would not be ignored. Ellison's people were making their presence known but

189

their visibility was now further limited by color. Because color was unimportant, it suddenly became all-important.

Cosby fired back with a full page ad in *Variety*: "Are we (comedians/actors) to be denied a right to romp through hotels, bite noses, and, in general, beat up one another in the way Abbott and Costello, Laurel and Hardy, Martin and Lewis, Buster Keaton and Charlie Chaplin did—and more recently as those actors in the movie, *Animal House*?

"I heard no cries of racism in those reviews. If my work is not funny—it's not funny. But this industry does not need projected racism from critics."

And Pryor quipped on a *Tonight Show* appearance, "It's white people who have found this offensive. They got their consciousness all of a sudden. We in no way meant to be anything but funny."

The censors were on the loose again. This time they were restricting Cosby and Pryor in an attempt to "protect" the image of the black people who had been so sorely wronged by the movie industry over the years. It was like the Klan protecting Malcolm X from racist slurs. It was absurd!

Pryor was right, whites, and a healthy sprinkling of so-called black people, had found a strange race consciousness which had searched out a way to fight racism—"kill off everybody who would remind you of the problem." It was like curing cancer by silencing the doctors who would say it exists.

The pressure was still on, and Pryor, after a trip to Africa, vowed never to use The Word again, saying, "the word is really like a branding iron and when you bring it out in the open and examine it you see it's nothing. If I can do something to help get its usage stopped,

I'd appreciate that."

Why the sudden turnabout?

Pryor explains, "To call a person a nigger is to call him something less than human . . . Don't call me no nigger because you're calling me nothing; and I am somebody . . . Think of how we refer to a black woman as a black bitch but you never hear of a white bitch. We've got to stop the name calling period so we learn to talk to each other and find out what the real problems are! I've grown to a new place."

The absurdity was still rooted in perception. Whites, and many blacks, couldn't "see the forest for the trees," or "separate the part from the whole." Niggers were either not-niggers, or they were niggers. In other words if white people were supposed to see black folks as being human, do it right, don't show no other kind of black to them, they can't handle the pressure of trying to tell them apart. All black folks still look alike, even if they are human!

Pryor shelved The Word that had made him famous but he didn't cop out, just as he didn't cop out about what happened New Year's Eve. He changed other people's attitudes as to what they were seeing. He did what he did, sure, changed his mind, but he did it. Didn't nobody make him do it. It is important for Pryor to be able to make that distinction.

"It served its purpose," Pryor said, returning from Kenya. "I'm not trying to undo anything because I didn't do anything wrong. ("I thought it was fair!" he said of his shooting a car on New Year's.) But I know I can do better."

He was doing all right as it was, even though he took a few shots from very color conscious people. The film *Richard Pryor Live In Concert* had turned a healthy

$350,000 a week to become the highest earning "live" movie of all time. He had come a long way since the days of *Wattstax*.

Pryor made his debut as a producer with the film *Family Dreams* for Universal Studios. Michael Glick handled the co-producing chores on the film based on an original idea by Pryor.

Pryor, Roger L. Simon and Lonnie Elder III put their talents together to fashion a script that was good enough to attract Cicely Tyson, an actress Pryor had always wanted to work with but was afraid to ask.

Attorney David Franklin had Ms. Tyson flown into Atlanta for a special screening of Pryor's *In Concert*. "I was amazed at my reaction to it," Tyson said, on the set of *Family Dreams*. "I mean, he is—needless to say—a person who uses four-letter words . . . But somehow when he uses them it takes it out of that realm.

"I realized," she said, "that part of his charm, part of his ability to win audiences was this kind of material. It's like he's a little boy who has heard all the swear words and has seen all the obscene gestures and has no idea of what they mean, but uses them just to be bad!"

Tyson was impressed with the actor/comic, especially after she had worked with him. "One of the things I learned about him," Tyson said, "is that he's a very generous and giving human. The reason I believe he appears sometimes to be in turmoil is because his sensitivities are all raw, they're all exposed, open, and are affected by everything and everyone . . . and that's just part of his genius."

Family Dreams is a romantic drama that finds Pryor, as Joe Braxton, a con man, driving a bus load of disadvantaged children and their teacher, Tyson, on a cross-country junket. It is a very un-Pryorish film some will say. But the truth is that anything in life, from birth to death, is meat for Pryor's art.

The film provided extensive work for blacks and women as technicians and creators. Roberta Flack was hired to sing the score.

David Franklin and William Greaves acted as co-executive producers on the film which was budgeted at $6 million dollars.

In early 1980 Pryor and Gene Wilder teamed up once more in a Sidney Poitier-produced film, *Stir Crazy*, for Columbia Pictures.

Stir Crazy, filmed at Arizona State Prison near Tucson, is described as an off-the-wall comedy about two transplanted New Yorkers whose shining dream of finding fame and fortune in America's Southwestern Sun Belt turns into a tarnished nightmare of prison life when a would-be playwright, Skip Donahue (Gene Wilder) and his friend, Harry Monroe (Pryor), an unemployed actor, are framed for bank robbery.

"The warden told me the movie will be good for morale," said Poitier, directing his first film in three years. "We will employ several hundred inmates."

And about the movie, Poitier told Bob Lucas of *Jet*, "The funniest!" And of Pryor? "Well, he's obviously a genius, and when he works he is usually very funny. But for some reason when you pair him with Gene Wilder, they make a particular kind of magic together. And, together, they are probably the funniest pair that's ever been on screen."

Pryor said, "I think what's happening with Gene and I, as a combination, is something you couldn't have predicted. A white guy and a black guy comedy team—you couldn't have made it up. It's like the people made it up in *Silver Streak*."

But Pryor can do nothing at all without stirring up some controversy. During the filming of *Stir Crazy*, it was reported that Pryor walked off the set saying, "I'm sick of the film business."

The word got out that nothing serious was going down. Pryor was a little under the weather, and there was some minor problem with a member of the crew. Pryor had not flipped out again. He was in control and working like the real professional he had proven himself to be over and over again. Still, doomsayers hovered above the comic, like great hungry vultures, and waiting for him to make the fatal mistake that would finally destroy him.

They didn't have long to wait.

The Monkey looked up with teary eyes,
Said, "Mr. Lion, I apologize,
you may as well stop beatin',
ain't no use in tryin',
No mother fucker's gon' stop my signifyin'."

10

Chapter 10: Oooooops!

"I put all that stuff—the cocaine, shooting my wife's car, and so forth—into the routine because people are thinking about it and they'd consider it strange if I didn't mention it. I had to say to myself, 'Now look, man, it happens to everybody; it just seems like it's happening more to you because it's been in the paper.' It would be hypocritical, otherwise. Am I going to act like I'm perfect and everybody else is an ass? You, know, I can be an ass, too!"

Pryor is a "rebounder," a tough man on the "boards." You can count on him to muff a shot, fuck up even, but he always makes that second shot a winner. It's an uncanny talent he has for bouncing back, for beating the odds, for defying everything and everyone— even death.

In many respects Pryor is a daredevil. No, I doubt that you'd ever catch Pryor sky diving, it was a long time before he got over his fear of flying. But Pryor would face down a klansman, would dozen-play with the sheeted horror, and extend the offer to "Kiss my black ass!" without flinching.

Rebel, daredevil, somehow they mean the same where Pryor is concerned. He tips into those dark rooms and closets we all avoid and checks things out, faces things, and takes some of the sting out of what he faces, what was once so frightening and threatening, by stripping it down and looking at it with the cold eye of the comedian.

"I just found out something, sometimes women don't have orgasms. That fucked me up! I thought I was doing some serious fuckin'. I'm talkin' 'bout when you get the hump in your back and shit, get all ugly in the face, sweat be dripping down."

Pryor could dish it out and Pryor could take it. He had talked himself out of jail a couple of times, and did his time when his mouth couldn't pull his ass free. He faced down the big "D"—death, suffered through the one thing Americans fear more than niggers and cancer, a heart attack. He survived. Snapped back like a young strong sapling that would only bend so far before saying, "Fuck it!"

Pryor is no Macho Man. He would be the first to agree with that. But he knows how to bob and weave, he knows how to slip a punch, and when the ass whuppin' is unavoidable, well, he can take that too. But always on his own terms.

The Pryor trademark is one of meekness laced heavily with cunning. There is a time to stand and talk shit and there is a time to run. Pryor knows the difference. He knows how to survive, save his own ass, without giving up too much ass in the process. He will go so far and no further.

It's uncanny the way Pryor has weathered adversity. Given the amount of drugs and booze he has allegedly taken into his system it is a miracle that he hasn't overdosed, driven into a mountain, or simply disintegrated. What holds Pryor up?

The black folk jumped down on him behind The Word. He didn't break or change until he felt it was time. That's the Pryor way of doing things.

He turned his back on Vegas, Hollywood and the people who said he would never work again, and worked and got rich enough to tell every damn body to "Kiss his black ass!"

But contrary to popular opinion, Pryor is generally very slective in choosing the targets for his artistic brick-bats. He wastes few words and gestures and is not afraid to throw a few missiles at himself. He'll laugh too.

On June 9, 1980, it seemed that Pryor's resiliency had been siphoned off, the great rebounder had lost his spring, there was no way he was going to survive his most recent indiscretion.

In a freak accident Richard Pryor became a flaming torch in a bedroom in his Northridge home. Pryor suffered third-degree burns over fifty percent of his upper torso, the news reports said. This time Pryor had really done himself in. The tongue-cluckers shook their heads and composed Pryor's obituary.

Dr. Jack Grossman, who treated Pryor at the burn center of Sherman Oaks Community Hospital, was solemn when he explained that Pryor had suffered burns on his face, abdomen, chest, back, both hands and right arm.

Pryor's condition, Grossman said, was "very guarded," because, statistically, persons in his age group have a twenty-five percent to thirty-five percent chance of survival. The faithful sent up a few prayers, puttin' in "emergency calls to God" on the critically burned Pryor's behalf. The lonely vigil began.

There were questions to be answered and Pryor was in no shape to do any talking. He was barely holding on to life. The speculators were alive with notions, possibilities. Still, there was no clearcut explanation of what had happened.

Rumor had it that Pryor told a doctor at the Sherman Oaks Community Hospital that he had been burned in a flareup of ether while "free basing," a process by which cocaine is purified into a more powerful product. It was the story that got to the press and it fit the Pryor profile. If anybody got messed up fooling with drugs Pryor would be a prime candidate. Hadn't he confessed his fondness for cocaine to a national television audience?

Most were ready to accept the initial report without challenge. It's the American way of doing things. Especially where rebels, people like Pryor, are concerned. It's easier that way.

Lt. Dan Cooke of the Los Angeles Police Department told the press that his investigation revealed that Pryor had told doctors that he was burned processing cocaine.

Gary Sawye, assistant executive director of the hospital, declined to say whether or not Pryor had made such a statement concerning "freebase."

Things were further complicated because police were unable to get into Pryor's fenced estate until the following morning after having a search warrant issued.

The search turned up nothing that would prove or disprove the "freebase" theory offered by the police or the story that the newspapers were pushing which said that a butane lighter "blew up" and sprayed Pryor with flaming liquid.

But as near as anyone has been able to tell, until Pryor decides to tell what he wants people to know, the chain of events started somewhere around the early evening hours on Monday, June 9.

The accident occurred somewhere in the sprawling Northridge estate occupied by Pryor and an elderly aunt, Jenny, who had come in from Peoria to stay with him. It was Aunt Jenny who smothered the flames that engulfed Pryor. But she was unable to hold him and he broke free and rushed out of his home and into the streets.

A patrol car spotted Pryor on a main street in his Northridge neighborhood. Neighbors and passersby were trying to talk to the injured comic who witnesses say was in "sheer agony" and mumbling in delirium.

Officer Richard Zielinski was the first policeman to reach Pryor. He observed that Pryor was in pain. His shirt was burned almost completely from his body. The officer was afraid to touch Pryor for fear of injuring him further.

In agony Pryor started jogging. The officer jogged with him, trying to talk to him, stop him.

"I can't stop, I can't stop!" Pryor is reported to have cried out. "I'll die if I stop!"

Pryor had been low-running, cool running, all his life. It looked as if he knew that if he slowed down at all he would die. It was probably that energy, that final burst of adrenalin which charged Pryor enough, or scared him enough, to make him fight back, even if it meant running. It probably seemed like the best thing to do at the time.

Fire officials arrived on the scene and after what papers reported to be a "violent struggle," during which Pryor is said to have exhorted, "C'mon, give me a second chance! I know I did wrong but I've got some good in me!" they controlled him.

Pryor was rushed to the burn center at the Sherman Oaks Community Medical Center. By 8:30 p.m. that Monday evening, Dr. Jack Grossman had begun resuscitative measures on the critically injured Pryor.

Reports that a butane lighter had blown up in Pryor's hand while he was trying to light a cigarette hit the news. There was confusion. What really happened? The free-basing story was juicier, more like Pryor. But the possibility that something as innocent as a cigarette lighter could have done the damage had its merits in fact.

Lt. Dan Cooke said, "No criminal charges will be filed because all there was was a statement. There's no evidence. There's no case."

Pryor had beaten the law. But it didn't seem that he would be able to beat death.

"He's lucky to be alive," said Dr. Jack Grossman. "He has been through a hell of a lot."

Almost immediately Pryor underwent special treatment in a hyperbaric chamber. The technique was one developed by Dr. Richard Grossman, brother of Dr. Jack Grossman. Said to speed healing by twenty fold, it involves sealing the patient in a tube, and then doubling or tripling atmospheric pressure, forcing oxygen into the blood.

Jim Brown, a close friend to Pryor, was on the set directing traffic, keeping things in hand. "He requested to see me. That's the only way I got in," said Brown. "He never mentioned pain. He's a very strong man. I didn't ask him what happened. We're close friends and I just didn't want to ask him about that."

David Franklin flew in from Atlanta and got the story straight. There was no way that he was going to allow the damaging "freebase" story to keep circulating.

"He said he was in his room and had a glass of rum," explained Franklin. "He bent over to light a cigarette and there was an explosion. That's what Richard told me."

Franklin insisted that he believed Pryor and that was the end of that. The man was in pain. The man was on the critical list. He could still die.

Pneumonia set in and threatened to beat Pryor down. "Because Richard has third-degree burns all the way around his upper body," said Grossman, "the injury acts as a leather tourniquet, restricting his breathing and normal coughing."

More experts were flown in. Pryor was getting the best. It was all up to him, up to the Gods and his innate resiliency. He was soon taken off the critical list. But doctors maintained that Pryor was still in very serious condition.

Said Grossman, "Burn patients are patients for life. We have patients who have been coming in for 10 or 15 years."

By late June Pryor had undergone operations to graft skin to his shoulders, back, chest, arms and neck. His face seemed to be healing on its own.

"He came through in fantastic shape," said Jim Brown, "and his condition has stabilized. We've been discussing things, talking about the future. Richard is thinking of some really important things to do."

If a new world can grow out of the ashes left by the destructive explosion of Mt. St. Helen's, it would seem possible that a man with Pryor's powers for recovery could pull a small rose from his own shit pile.

Redd Foxx spearheaded a 24-hour telethon in Pryor's honor. The money raised was donated to the burn center at the Sherman Oaks Community Medical Center and other needy burn centers throughout the nation.

Dr. Eugene Scott donated his television and radio facilities toward the benefit.

Close friends gathered around, swamped Pryor with their prayers, their cards, their presence. Ex-wives camped out in the waiting rooms. Superstars called and visited. Even Senator Ted Kennedy showed personal concern. It was as if a hero had fallen in battle.

The hospital's switchboard was burdened by calls from as far away as Australia. The wiry, wiley man from Peoria had managed to spread his shit wide if not deep.

"I'm going to fight it . . . I'm going to live," Brown quoted Pryor, who had gained strength and courage from all the well-wishers, from close friends like Stan Shaw who worked with Pryor on *Bingo Long*, Jennifer Lee who daily sent notes to Pryor's bedside.

If nothing else, Pryor found that he is loved. People do care about him. It's probably the most important thing in Pryor's life, to be respected, to know that people understand and care. Pryor cares. A $100,000 donation to the Charles R. Drew Post Graduate Medical School for research shows how much.

There is a special something that makes Pryor lovable, that makes him valuable. He has the ability, the gift if you will, for taking the pressure off. His insight allows him to see through to the heart of something and strip away those things that frighten.

Pryor lightens dark corners. He strips away the pretentious. He samples the poison for us, and then let's us know just how deadly the shit really is. Pryor is not a cult leader seeking followers to his way of life. Rather he uses his mistakes, his way of life, to light the way for others. He can do it. He knows when to duck and run.

After a visit to the hospital to see Pryor, Sammy Davis, Jr.—a rebounder in his own right—offered, "There's something happening in him—that survival thing; you can see it in his eyes and it's a beautiful thing to see. It makes one really feel like, 'What have you got to worry about?' "

Pryor has been to the very brink of death. He peeped into the swirling fires of hell and told the devil to "Kiss his ass!" he wasn't coming!

What did Pryor see? What new insights has he gained from his near fatal brush with fire and death, two demons which cower the longest?

David Franklin said that the ordeal really "scared" Pryor. Franklin says that Pryor is really a changed man. Another plateau? Or another sham?

Pryor plans a book. There is no doubt that it will be a best seller before it comes off the shelf. And then maybe the real truth will come out. Maybe Pryor is invulnerable!

ABOUT THE AUTHOR

Joseph Nazel is a prolific author of both fiction and nonfiction works. His previous biography for Holloway House, *Paul Robeson, Biography of a Proud Man,* was his first foray into the biographical genre, following the publication of fourteen novels.

Mr. Nazel has also been a magazine writer and editor, notably with *Players Magazine* where he enjoyed two stints as editor-in-chief, leaving both times to return to his first love, writing.

Mr. Nazel is a long-time resident of Los Angeles.

Knocks the lid off the lone assassin theory!

A Case of Conspiracy
by Michael Newton

JAMES EARL RAY AND THE ASSASSINATION OF MARTIN LUTHER KING, JR.

NONFICTION / On April 4, 1968, at 6:01 p.m., a shot rang out. The great civil rights leader, Rev. Martin Luther King Jr., fell to the floor with massive head and throat wounds. Death was almost instantaneous. After a manhunt that spanned the United States, Canada and Mexico, James Earl Ray was arrested sixty-five days later at London's Heathrow Airport and accused of being King's assassin. But was he? Only Ray's surprise guilty plea, which he later recanted, saved the prosecution from having to prove their case ■ ■ ■ In a carefully researched and gripping step-by-step reconstruction of the assassination and its aftermath, author Michael Newton raises new and troubling questions about the investigation, arrest and trial of James Earl Ray which suggest that a conspiracy did indeed exist and that Ray may not have been the assassin after all. In the process, the author exposes faulty investigative techniques, self-serving attorneys and most important, reveals James Earl Ray's character as never before. It's as exciting and puzzling as any mystery novel published in recent years.

The action-packed, inspiring story of a black basketball player who conquers heroin and the basketball court.

BIOGRAPHY Earl (The Goat) Manigault had what it takes to make it in pro basketball. He had the timing, he had the talent, he even had his own patented "double dunk" shot which nobody else could do. Earl also had one fatal weakness common to many of his friends in Harlem—the need to get high in order to forget the mean streets where he lived. Beginning with marijuana, going on to cocaine and graduating to heroin, his habit inevitably led to crime and he got caught. But, unlike so many men who get caught in a similar trap, Earl had the guts and the determination to go "cold turkey" and to rebuild his life. You can still find him on the streets of Harlem, coaching promising young basketball players and working to keep them from falling into the same trap that cost him a life of glory and riches.

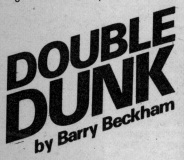 

DOUBLE DUNK by Barry Beckham

Full dramatic account of the people and events that led to the Muslim revolution in Iran and a frightening look into the future.

KHOMEINI

THE SHAH, THE AYATOLLAH, THE SHI'ITE EXPLOSION BY EDDIE STONE

NONFICTION / The Iranian revolution, led by the Ayatollah Ruhollah Khomeini, has dominated world headlines and the thoughts of free people everywhere. Who is this strange, mystic man who was able to topple a monarchy that had lasted 2500 years? Where did he come from? Where did he get his strange and terrible power? And even more important, where will it all lead? ■ ■ ■ This book takes a hard look at what's happening now and why. It explains the impact of the Muslim religion and the Shi'ite sect of Islam that Khomeini leads. It introduces you to the history of Persia and its shahs . . . a culture that was rocked to its core when oil riches enabled the Shah to propel a backward country into the twentieth century. It illuminates the stage of current events with startling detail and provides a frightening glimpse into the future. ■ ■ ■ You may not like what you see but see it you must, for what is happening now will shape your life and the life of all on this planet for decades to come. This book is must reading for anyone who hopes to understand events reported in the daily newspapers.

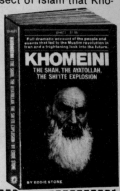

THE TRUE LIFE STORY OF THE GREATEST FIGHTER OF ALL TIME

MUHAMMAD ALI

by ROBERT HOSKINS

The world calls him the greatest and justly so. Golden Gloves Champion. Olympic Gold Medalist. Heavyweight Champion of the World—not once, not twice, but three times, Ali gained the ultimate boxing crown. The only man in history to accomplish this magnificent feat. It is no wonder that in a recent poll of high school students in the United States, Muhammad Ali was the only living man they considered to be a real hero ■ From his humble beginnings in the Deep South, where he was born Cassius Clay, Jr., before his famous conversion to the Black Muslim religion, Ali rose to be the foremost boxing champion the world has ever known. His boxing skill, combined with his fierce determination to succeed, has made him a true immortal in our time.

WITH 16 PAGES OF PHOTOS

THE TRUE LIFE STORY OF BASKETBALL'S MOST EXCITING PLAYER

DR. J

by D. Thomas

Julius Erving, known throughout his career as The Doctor because of the surgical precision with which he plays his game, has dominated the world of basketball during his over nine year professional career. Turning pro following his sophomore year at the University of Massachusetts, he joined the New York Nets of the ill-fated American Basketball Association, and led them to the league championship in 1976. That year saw the demise of the ABA, but not of Dr. J. ■ ■ ■ The following season he was traded to the Philadelphia 76ers, garnering for himself a $3.5 million six-year contract, in addition to the $3 million paid to the Nets for his contract. And in Philadelphia he has stayed, continuing to leap, soar, hover in the air, performing moves like no other basketball player in the world. There is only one Doctor. Dr. J. ■ ■ ■ With 16 pages of photos.

THE TRUE LIFE STORY OF BASKETBALL'S NEWEST SUPERSTAR

The 1979-80 National Basketball Association season was probably the most exciting and electrifying in recent years. A great deal of that excitement was due to the phenomenal rise to stardom of Earvin ''Magic'' Johnson, a rookie player with the Los Angeles Lakers who led his team to victory in the crucial, final game of the NBA Championship Playoffs following an injury to Kareem Abdul-Jabar which eliminated him from the game. ■ Magic Johnson's rocketship ride to superstardom is unequalled in modern times. From Lansing, Michigan, where he led his high school basketball team to a state championship, he went to Michigan State, where he performed his magic act twice with two state championships. ■ It was then that he made the decision to turn pro with the Lakers after the completion of his sophomore year in college. The rest is history—with many pages still to be written. ■ With 16 pages of photos!

MAGIC JOHNSON
by J. Dodd

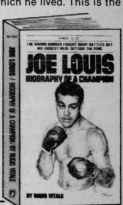

JESSE JACKSON

BIOGRAPHY OF AN AMBITIOUS MAN

BY EDDIE STONE

BIOGRAPHY / He is the most talked about black leader of today. He dared black Americans to stand on their feet. He uncovered the hidden prejudice and discrimination of the North. Chicago's powerful Mayor Daley fought him with every bit of strength he had. Millions watched as he appeared on the Today Show in a sweater freshly stained with Martin Luther King's blood. An organizer. A do-or-die, ambition-driven and courageous Jesse Jackson emerged to pick up the reins of black power when Dr. King tragically left his people. As Dr. King led in the 50s and 60s, Jackson leads irrefutably in the 70s and 80s. His story reaches out to all men, to all races and hopes ... for the new tomorrow.

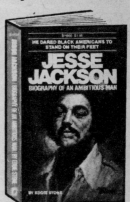

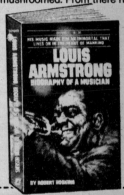

ANDREW YOUNG
BIOGRAPHY OF A REALIST

BY EDDIE STONE

BIOGRAPHY / Impatient and frustrated in his efforts to secure world peace and justice, Andrew Young resigned his post as U.S. ambassador to the United Nations after a breach of protocol embarrassed Israeli-American policy over the Palestine Liberation Organization. But that step in his career should prove to be only a pause in his meteoric rise to world prominence. Young's life has been characterized by his work for the good of all men, although his beginnings would not have presaged his life to come. After giving up an uninvolved middle class existence to become a minister, Andrew Young joined forces with Martin Luther King to fight on the front lines of the civil rights movement, quickly becoming a respected black leader in is own right. Credited with delivering the black vote for President Carter in 1976, Young will undoubtedly continue to have a powerful influence in the world political arena for many years to come. Andrew Young—realist, mediator, and spokesman for his people—is above all a fascinating character brought into sharp focus by author Eddie Stone.

PAUL ROBESON
BIOGRAPHY OF A PROUD MAN
BY JOSEPH NAZEL

BIOGRAPHY / Paul Robeson—proud, defiant, beloved, reviled, misunderstood, idolized—was above all a man of principle, whose deep and abiding love for his people was the driving force in his life. ■ By refusing to play the stereotypical roles offered him by Hollywood, he spurned fabulous riches available to very few of his race. By championing the rights of black people the world over and recognizing their roots in Africa years before the word Afro-American was coined, he created controversy that swirled around his head for decades. By defying the infamous House on Un-American Activities Committee, he proved the power of his principles while dooming himself to an ever-diminishing income. Even after death, controversy continued over his star in Hollywood's Walk of Fame. ■ Overcoming racial prejudice was more important to him than material considerations, even though his lifelong crusade to stamp out racism ultimately cost him his career and his health. But his pride remained intact until the very end. He became a legend in his own time and remains today a hero to black people the world over.

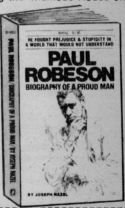

BOOK ORDER FORM

Dear Reader:

You'll find many other books of interest listed on previous pages. If they are not now available at your book dealer, we will be delighted to rush your order by direct mail. Fill in form below and mail with your remittance.

SPECIAL ORDER BOOK DEPT.
8060 MELROSE AVE. • LOS ANGELES, CA 90046

Please send me the following books I have listed by Number:

_____   _____   _____   _____

_____   _____   _____   _____

_____   _____   _____   _____

_____   _____   _____   _____

I enclose 50 cents additional per order to cover postage on all orders under $5.00 (California residents please add 6% sales tax).

Enclosed is $_____ ☐ cash, ☐ check, ☐ money order payment in full for all books ordered above (sorry no C.O.D.'s). ☐ I am over 21.

Name _____

Address _____

City _____ State _____ Zip _____